COLLEGE FOR SALE

COLLEGE FOR SALE

The Fall and Rise of a Closed College Campus

RICHARD E. SCHNEIDER

iUniverse, Inc.
Bloomington

It was an institution for children of the middle class ...
a good post–World War II college that specialized
in generating more citizenry for the middle class.

—Philip McLaughlin
Nasson College, class of 1975

CONTENTS

List of Illustrations ix

Introduction xi

1. The End. 1
   Marketing the School Before It Closed. 3
   Marketing the School After It Closed 4
   The First Auction: 1984. 14

2. Nasson College Is Saved 17
   What Might Have Been and What Was 26
   Other Campus Buildings Find New Life. 28
   The Alumni Association Hangs On 28
   Nasson College Operations. 30
   The Accreditation Problem 32
   Nasson College: Open for Business. 34
   The New Nasson College Begins to Fall Apart. 35
   The Alumni Association Struggles to Survive 36
   Use of Other Buildings 37
   Nasson College Looks for Its Own Identity 39

3. A Pot of Gold. 43
   Past Deeds Begin to Close In on Mattar 48
   What to Do with the Campus?. 49

4. The Second Auction: 1996 55

5. UNE Comes to the Rescue. 59
   The Alumni Association Gets a Home Base 61

6. The Third Auction: 1997 85
    The Nasson Heritage Center 94

7. The Springvale Public Library Comes to the Rescue 97
    Plans for Other Campus Buildings 99

8. Alumni Activities Soar 103

9. The Nasson Community Center 109
    The Day So Big It Took Two Nights!. 116
    The Community Center Opens. 117
    The Little Theatre at Nasson 118
    The Fall of Edward Mattar 120

10. The Rest of the Campus Gets Developed. 123
    The 1971 Time Capsule. 124

11. The Magic That Is Nasson 127

Appendix A: Sources and Acknowledgments. 131

Appendix B: The Lawsuits and Administrative Decisions . . . 133

Appendix C: The Accreditations and Recognitions of
            Nasson College. 134

Appendix D: The Accreditations and Recognitions of
            (New) Nasson College and/or Nasson Institute . 135

Appendix E: Presidents of the Nasson College Alumni
            Association since the Closing of the School . . . 136

Index 137

LIST OF ILLUSTRATIONS

Following page 63

a. The campus, early 1970s
b. Nasson College 75th Commencement, 1989
c. Brown Hall, 1997
d. The Little Theatre, 1999
e. Interior, the Memorial Student Activity Center, 2002
f. The college "quad," 1999
g. The quad, after demolition of Allen Hall and the dining commons, 2001
h. The Little Theatre, 2001
i. Brown Hall, 2000
j. Kids' basketball in the newly renovated gym
k. The Nasson College Alumni Flag Plaza
l. Alumni website announces parade
m. Nasson Alumni homecoming parade, 2004
n. Southern end of the quad, May 2001
o. Southern end of the quad, October 2001
p. Seacoast Career Schools graduation in the gym
q. Opening of the Nasson Heritage Center in 1998
r. Brown Hall, restored to glory
s. The Little Theatre today
t. The campus today

Introduction

This book follows the path laid by its predecessor, *Nasson: The Seventy Years*, by Albert L. Prosser and Richard D'Abate. No doubt, when Captain Prosser finished his manuscript in 1975, he expected the school to continue on for many years, if not forever. After all, with his final chapter, titled "Nasson Restored to Normalcy," it seemed that the problems the school had in the late 1960s were finally behind it. But as Mr. D'Abate so thoroughly chronicled, the school's real problems were just beginning. So when Mr. D'Abate finished his manuscript with the closing of the school in 1983, no doubt he, and most everyone else, expected that really was the end of the story.

It may have been the end of the college, but it was hardly the end of the story. Most colleges that close seem to go quietly, their assets sold off and their buildings torn down or converted to other uses. But, as we know, that was not what happened to Nasson.

It is this later story that is the subject of this tome. And the end of Nasson is still not written.

— RES

1

THE END

On April 30, 1983, Robert "Stoney" Stone, Nasson College Class of 1972, was elected president of the Nasson College Alumni Association. The next day, the college went out of business. "It was not my fault!" he would insist over the years.

Indeed it wasn't. The path to closure had been set in motion many years before, long before the college filed for bankruptcy in November 1982.

Nasson College's history was too brief. It began in 1912 as Nasson Institute, a two-year program for women. It became a four-year college in 1935 and went coed in 1952. After admitting men, Nasson quickly grew into a well-respected, four-year, accredited liberal arts college, reaching a student enrollment of over nine hundred in the late 1960s. Nasson offered majors in such fields as biology, English, environmental science, government, history, mathematics, medical technology, and many other subjects.

The school was located in Springvale, a village in the town of Sanford, Maine. Sanford was, by the 1960s, a classic rust belt community, where the mills that had employed thousands of workers in good-paying jobs throughout the first half of the twentieth century had closed in the 1950s. And though the town's efforts at redevelopment earned it the nickname of "The Town That Refused to Die," it struggled mightily.[1] Then in the mid-1970s, some federal urban renewal money became available, and for reasons few today can fathom, the town took the money and proceeded to tear down most of the storefront businesses in Springvale and Sanford. The

---

1   Today, the town is diversified, with more than forty firms producing a vast array of
     items from woolens to aircraft and their components.

spirit of both the town and the village was destroyed, and neither location ever fully recovered.

The Nasson College campus was located right in the heart of Springvale. It was a lovely, classic New England small college. If Hollywood had been looking for a setting for a small college, Nasson would have been perfect. It had buildings old and new, a well-equipped library, a large gymnasium and a little theater, a science center greater than anyone might expect to find on such a small campus, and lots of dormitories.

And it had lots of debt, since many of the newest buildings had been built with borrowed money, most of it federal. Those debts eventually caught up with the school. By the 1970s, weak management, changing demographics, the end of the military draft, and repeated poor planning led to seriously declining enrollment. The school's business model was financed almost completely by current students' tuition and fees. When the number of students dropped, so did the income.[2] The school eventually went broke, filed for Chapter 11 bankruptcy,[3] and closed in 1983.[4]

Of course, everyone at the school did everything they could to save the school. For example, in the years before the end, the administration—hoping to attract prospective students and recognizing that long-deferred maintenance had left much of the campus looking rather shabby—refurbished the entire campus, buildings, and grounds, inside and out.[5] The idea was to make the school look healthy and inviting to prospective students. It was said that the campus looked better on the day the school closed than it had in many previous years. Although this effort did not really do anything to save the school, the unintended effect was that it may have helped preserve the buildings and grounds for what would be a long dormant period.

---

2   Ninety percent of the school's operating funds was derived from student tuition and fees. Each year, any operating shortage was carried forward and repaid with tuition from the new year. When enrollment for the fall of 1982 proved to be much smaller than expected, Key Bank, the school's chief financial base, canceled the college's line of credit. That left a severe cash deficiency; the school would not have enough cash to make it through the fall semester. Bankruptcy was the only way to stave off disaster and the chaos of a midyear closing.

3   Once the college declared bankruptcy, one of the board's main focuses was to secure permission from the court to complete the academic year for current students. The board accomplished its goal, allowing for the orderly completion of the academic year, graduation for seniors, and orderly transfer for underclassmen.

4   For a thoroughly detailed explanation of why the college closed, see Albert L. Prosser and Richard D'Abate, *Nasson: The Seventy Years* (West Kennebunk, ME: Phoenix Publishing, 1993).

5   Prosser and D'Abate, *The Seventy Years*, 199.

Thus, as the school limped toward closing, the main part of the campus, at least, was in reasonably good shape. Because of that, many felt that the campus would still have a successful future, if not as a college, then as some other educational or business site.

And yet not everyone in town was sad to see the college close. Ronald LaFerriere, executive director of the Sanford-Springvale Chamber of Commerce, said that no one was too upset about the possibility of Nasson closing, except for, perhaps, some of the merchants in Springvale.[6]

Not so, said Edgar Schick, president of the college when it closed. According to Schick, closing the college would cost the community about $20 million, because not only would the school's ninety employees lose their jobs, local businesses would lose customers and sales.

Or not. When the college was fully operating, an estimated $10 million circulated in payroll and purchases. But by the time the college closed, it had little economic impact on the town.[7] Of note, in the 1950 Nasson College yearbook, *The Nugget*, there were advertisements for twenty-four businesses in Springvale. In the 1970 *Nugget*, there were thirteen. In the 1981 Nugget, there were only three.

MARKETING THE SCHOOL BEFORE IT CLOSED

Even before the school held its final graduation, college officials tried to market the school. According to Steve Morris, chairman of the board of trustees during Nasson's final year, the board did try to find a successor institution.[8] The hope was that education might go on, if not as an independent Nasson College, then perhaps as a branch campus of another school, something like Nasson College of the University of Southern Maine or the Nasson Campus of New England College or of New Hampshire College, or something like that.

One of the people Morris talked to between 1982 and '83 was the president of the University of Southern Maine, Bob Woodberry. Morris said Nasson offered Woodberry a turnkey operation, complete with beds in the dormitories, books in the library, coffee in the dining hall, and students ready to go. All USM needed to do was come in and assume Nasson's debt, which was "minimal,"[9] and the university would have the Springvale

---

6   Julie L'Heureux, "Closing Feared," *The Sanford News*, October 26, 1982.

7   "Reaction to Mattar Plan Mixed," *Portland Press Herald*, December 14, 1984.

8   Steve Morris (chairman of Nasson College's board of trustees during the school's final year), in interview with the author, January 19, 2012.

9   The short-term debt at the time was about $600,000. The long-term debt was $1.4

Campus of the University of Southern Maine or the Nasson Campus of the University of Southern Maine. Morris thought Nasson had a pretty convincing argument. York County, where Springvale was located, was the fastest growing county in Maine, and the University of Maine System did not have a presence in York County at that time. Morris thinks USM liked the idea, but USM had just consolidated what had been the Portland and Gorham Campuses of the University of Maine under the University of Southern Maine banner. Woodberry already had some problems with that merger, so to take on the Nasson campus in York County at that time would have been too much to handle.

MARKETING THE SCHOOL AFTER IT CLOSED

Nasson College ended its educational activities on May 1, 1983. But while classes had ended, corporate activity at Nasson continued. The board of trustees continued to meet; the office of the registrar remained open on an "as needed" basis to handle students' transcript requests and other business. Remaining on the payroll were one dean, one principal business officer, and three other members of the school's staff.[10] However, once the students left in May and all known options for a partnership with another school were exhausted, the driver of all events soon became the lawyers (Verrill & Dana and Pierce Atwood). In a very real sense, operational control and the fate of the college from that point on was in the hands of the attorneys.

Allen Mapes was treasurer of the board when the school closed. Like Morris, Mapes believed that another school would be interested in the facility because he felt Nasson was a gem. Perhaps a school would want to grab the place, or a research and development branch of a major corporation might be interested. Mapes even talked about moving the state prison there and building a wall around the main part of the campus. They were just looking for some way of bringing life back to the campus. Mapes said he never dreamed it would be closed forever. [11]

One encouraging prospect arose soon after closing. The Training and

---

million, though the college had assets of about $8 to $10 million (minutes of the Nasson Alumni Council Meeting, November 13, 1982). In 2011 dollars, that would be about $1.4 million, $3.2 million, and $19 to $23 million respectively (Bureau of Labor Statistics, CPI Inflation Calculator).

10 *Nasson College v. NEASC*, 80 B.R. 600 (1988) at 602 [*see infra*, n.138]; Nasson College, *Welcome Back* (apparently a special publication of Nasson College), September 3, 1985, 13.

11 Allen Mapes (treasure of Nasson College's board of trustees when the school closed), in interview with the author, January 20, 2012.

Development Corporation of Bangor, Maine, expressed interest. TDC's plan was to provide a two- and four-year liberal arts program, a business and industry training program, and a convention center. The school hoped to start up in September 1984, if all funding was in place. The school would employ about 150 people and retain the name Nasson College.

The school negotiated with the US Bankruptcy Court and obtained an option on the property. TDC needed a financial package worth $7.2 million to run the college. Much of that was to pay off the debts and meet Nasson's obligations. The rest of the money was to give the college the ability to stay in business for the next four or five years that TDC estimated it would take to actually begin to make a profit. TDC had already committed $3.1 million to the project and hoped to raise an additional $2 million in the next ninety days. TDC formally asked the town of Sanford to prepare a $1.5 million Urban Development Action Grant for the takeover of Nasson College.[12] TDC also asked Sanford to purchase the school's old library and its contents for $500,000 and then lease it to TDC for $1 a year. However, in order to obtain a UDAG grant, TDC needed to get the approval of the town through a town-meeting vote. In addition, a town-meeting vote would be needed for the town to spend $500,000 on the library.[13]

TDC received a $500,000 pledge from a major computer company. Then in November 1983, TDC announced that it was seeking a $3 million loan from Canal Bank and Trust Co. The town-meeting members approved the UDAG request and voted to acquire the library by a vote of 88–2.[14]

In the meantime, the state and the town were considering other options for the Nasson campus. In January 1984, an ad hoc committee was formed by Governor Joseph Brennan to determine the potential of redeveloping the school and how that redevelopment would benefit taxpayers.[15] The committee consisted of Chairman Les Stephens of the State Development Office; Wayne Ross of the Southern Maine Vocational Technical Institute;

---

12   Kim Clark, "Training Firm Seeks Town's Help," *Sanford News*, Aug 9, 1983, 1; Nason College, *Welcome*, 13.

13   The town of Sanford, prior to 2004, had a town-meeting form of government. The flow of legislation and appropriations went something like this: The town administrator submitted a proposal to the board of selectmen. If the selectmen approved the proposal, the board would move it to the warrant committee, which was the financial center of the town government. The warrant committee would submit it to the town-meeting. The town-meeting members, elected by residential wards, had the final say. From time to time, a unit could hold a special meeting, out of order.

14   Nasson College, *Welcome*, 13; "State Must Help Nasson 'Before It's Too Late'," *Sanford News*, March 6, 1984.

15   Nasson College, *Welcome*, 13.

and Robert Borgeault, executive director of the Employment Training Program in the Maine Department of Labor. Their mission was to evaluate all options, including the TDC plan. Sanford hired Meredith & Grew, Inc., a Boston-based, full-service real estate firm. The firm was to oversee a regional and national marketing study in an effort to find a suitable use for the campus.

Members of the Brennan Committee (named for the governor) traveled to Nasson and met with college trustees. They talked with local residents, merchants, and town officials. The response was generally consistent; the facility should remain an educational institution.

One result of the committee's work was finding that Job Training Partnership Act funds were already committed elsewhere. This meant that TDC, which had been counting on those funds to be used as collateral for the $3 million loan from Canal Bank, would be unable to meet the bank's requirements. As an alternative, the committee considered reconstituting Nasson through shared usages or cooperative combined uses. For example, state agencies and educational institutions could share use of the facilities, at least for part of the year. In the meantime, Stephen Horan, vice president of Meredith and Grew, said that while TDC was not out of the picture, M&G had to be prepared to move forward if the TDC proposal did not work out.[16]

The Brennan Committee held a public hearing in Sanford on February 28, 1984. About twenty-five members of the public attended, several of whom urged that the campus not be sold at public auction to developers who might turn it into housing.[17] Some voiced support for the TDC plan, and many strongly supported the idea of making the campus a part of the state university system.

Many townspeople missed the school. Jack Allen, president of the Sanford-Springvale Merchants Association, reported that, since the school had closed the previous May, three businesses had declined in Springvale. Because the school had closed, $1.5 to $1.75 million in salaries alone were lost. Others noted that local citizens missed the school's activities, such as publications, art displays, and performing-arts presentations. Students in secondary schools, blue-collar workers, and businessmen who wanted to expand their skills and knowledge also missed the school.[18]

---

16   Maureen Milliken, "Firm Hired to Sell Vacant Campus," *Journal Tribune*, February 28, 1984; S. Scott Hoar, "Nasson Advertising for Buyer," *Portland Press Herald*, February 28, 1984, 13.

17   C. Scott Hoar, "State Urged to Help Preserve Educational Role for Campus," *Portland Press Herald*, February 29, 1984.

18   Nasson College, *Welcome*, 13.

But the pieces of the TDC plan did not fall into place. The bank wanted a market study before it would commit to a $3 million loan, but the study would cost $100,000. TDC could not afford that.[19] Alternatively, the school believed that, if it was able to obtain Job Training Partnership Act contracts, it would be allowed to skip the market study. While the Ford Foundation did choose TDC to be the sole technical assistant to its Comprehensive Competiveness Program, other contracts did not materialize.[20]

Another blow was that the Department of Housing and Urban Development issued a policy statement that educational institutions did not qualify as aiding a town's economy.[21] That meant that TDC was not eligible for the UDAG grant. (TDC appealed that determination, and while it did eventually prevail on appeal, the decision came too late to help the training center.)

Finally, TDC gave up. Charles Tetro, president of TDC, said that, although the company still had an interest in taking over the campus, it had to suspend its efforts.[22]

The Brennan Committee considered another approach. If there was no one entity that could use the entire campus, then the committee would consider parceling it out to different organizations that only needed a smaller place.[23] Perhaps the University of Southern Maine, Southern Maine Vocational-Technical Institute, and/or other private organizations might use the campus for satellite programs. The schools could share the library and Science Center and even dormitories and offices.[24]

Sanford's warrant committee members had another idea. In May 1984, they suggested that the town-meeting appoint a committee to study the town's potential role in the sale of the college. They wanted to know the town's options to acquire the campus in case efforts to reopen the college failed.[25] At the same time, the town tried to market the campus. "For sale: 1 college, price negotiable" ran the headline on a *Boston Globe* article.[26]

19   Maureen Milliken, "Brennen Panel Holds Nasson Project Fate," Outlook (Biddeford, Maine), February 20, 1984.

20   Milliken, "Brennen Panel."

21   "Nasson Options Studied," *Sanford News*, January 31, 1984.

22   Maureen Milliken, "TCD Drops Nasson Takeover Proposal, But Door Isn't Shut," *Journal Tribune*, March 13, 1984.

23   Maureen Milliken, "State Job Training Funds Out of Nasson Picture," *Journal Tribune*, March 10, 1984.

24   C. Scott Hoar, "Nasson Efforts Please Miller," *Portland Press Herald*, June 13, 1984.

25   Nasson College, *Welcome*, 13.

26   Peter Anderson, "For Sale: 1 College, Price Negotiable," *The Boston Globe*, May 20,

The package could include the gym, the library (which still contained 131,000 books), the Science Center, the theater, the dormitories, the central campus, the woods, and the pond. There were mattresses, books, test tubes, and everything a small college needed. All together, there were nineteen buildings and 240 acres.[27] You could have it all for a mere $3.7 million. A Portland real estate firm appraised the property at more than $9 million. Morris, who was still officially chairman of the board of trustees, said the board would sell for even less than the asking price, if the right organization came along.

Curiously, a year after Nasson closed, the word had not gotten around to everyone. That second summer after closing, six hundred high school students actually applied for admission to the school for the fall of 1985.[28] Of course, experience showed that, even if they all could have been accepted, the students' actual registration rate would have been only a small fraction of the 600.

In the midst of all this, in the fall of 1984, Nasson alumni set up a tent on the quad, and about twenty alumni gathered to celebrate homecoming, as they had always done, and as they would (hopefully) continue to do.[29]

As the May 1984 Sanford town-meeting approached, no buyer for Nasson had come forward. Now, a year after closing, Nasson's creditors were expected to initiate liquidation (auction) proceedings. Still, the creditors came to the town with a proposal to avoid the auction. The idea was to have the town lease the gymnasium, the dining commons, the library, Reed Hall, Alumni Hall, the Little Theatre, and Shaw Field. The lease would run from August 1, 1984, to May 31, 1985, for $146,000.[30] The funds would be used to help defray the costs of maintenance and operations of the campus while efforts continued to market the campus. The library would be open to the public, at least for a few hours each day. The gym would be open, and the Little Theatre and dining commons might be used.[31]

The idea was debated at a special town-meeting. Proponents argued that the money would buy time to find a buyer, which would prevent the assets from being liquidated at a public auction, at least until the summer of 1985. The consultants, Meredith & Grew, would still have a year to

---

1984.

27 Hoar, "Nasson Advertising."

28 Anderson, "For Sale."

29 Stoney, "Homecoming 2000," *Nasson News*, 3 (Winter 2001).

30 Nasson College, *Welcome*, 15; C. Scott Hoar, Commentary, "Nasson Plan Proves Hot Discussion," *Portland Press Herald*, July 4, 1984.

31 "Nasson Lease Could Buy Necessary Time," *Sanford News*, July 7, 1983.

continue searching for a buyer, and the state committee would have more time to try to implement plans for creating an education park at Nasson. Some thought it was a wise investment, a way to avoid auctioning off the campus. To let the auction proceed and have the campus broken up would be shortsighted, they said. Opponents argued that the $146,000 would basically go to the creditors without the town receiving anything tangible in return. Moreover, if any of the buildings were leased to the town, then the town would be responsible for any heating, electrical, maintenance, insurance, and security costs, which were estimated at $340,000 a year.[32] Still, when the proposal got to the selectmen, they voted in favor of the plan, 3 to 2.[33]

Speakers on both sides of the issue engaged in a lengthy debate at a meeting in July 1984. But by a vote of 14 to 3, the warrant committee rejected the plan. The prevailing sense was that the money would just be a gift to the college creditors, and there was no guarantee that the extra time would restore Nasson College. Some said that the town would be setting a bad precedent by giving a grant to a private, nonprofit college— which technically still existed—to maintain the property.[34] There were no alternatives offered. Town Administrator David Miller said that the town could not just lend the college money, and buying parts of the campus did not solve the problem.[35]

At the town-meeting on August 7, 1984, opponents won out. A total of 113 of the town's 147 voting representatives attended, and the majority voted against the lease plan.[36]

Officials still had hopes that someone would come forward to buy or lease the campus. There were six to ten prospective purchasers, including representatives of two foreign groups who visited the campus in August.[37] The University of Southern Maine operated a branch school in the Village Shoppes on Main Street in Springvale, but when its lease was up, it still declined to rent any of the Nasson campus. According to Lorraine Masure, there were inquiries from numerous sites for relocation, but USM would

32 "W.C. Questions Merits of Lease," *Sanford News*, July 17, 1984.

33 C. Scott Hoar, "Selectmen Endorse Draft of Lease," *Portland Press Herald*, July 20, 1984.

34 Nasson College, *Welcome*, 15; Linc Bedrosian, "Auction Block Next Step if TM Nixes College Lease," *Sanford News*, July 24, 1984.

35 C. Scott Hoar, Analysis, "Sanford Residents Seek Alternative," *Portland Press Herald*, July 25, 1984.

36 C. Scott Hoar, "Sanford Rejects Nasson Pay Plan," *Portland Press Herald*, August 8, 1984; Ged Carbone, "Nasson Future Left to Hang on Auction Sale," *Journal Tribune*, August 8, 1984.

37 Hoar, "Sanford Residents Seek."

not consider moving to Nasson.[38] When USM announced its intention to move to the vacant Don's Electric building, town code enforcement officer Brian Howard ruled that that location was not zoned for a school.[39] Alice O'Brian, the school's community relations director, then said that USM was not opposed to moving into Nasson as part of a sharing arrangement. USM was ready to move, but the campus plan required negotiations with numerous entities.

Sanford selectmen held a special meeting in August to appoint Portland attorney Richard Poulis, a former bankruptcy judge, to be the town's legal representative in Nasson's bankruptcy proceedings.[40] Poulis's assignment was to protect whatever interests the town might have in the school. Selectmen believed that the town should have a say in the time period for liquidation, if it came to that. They wanted to avoid a public auction because they felt that there were interested parties that would buy the college if they had more time.

But as a result of the rejection of the one-year lease idea, the creditors immediately began proceedings to have a public auction of Nasson's assets.[41] On September 18, 1984, Nasson's creditors' committee, which represented more than seven hundred creditors that had claims against Nasson, filed a liquidation plan for the school. Auctioneers were sought, with the public auction to be held by Thanksgiving 1984.[42]

In October 1984, Becker Junior College of Worcester, Massachusetts was reported to be looking for an alternative site.[43] Becker had a total enrollment of 1,300 students, with 750 at its main campus and 550 more at its branch campus in Leicester, Massachusetts.[44] The school was looking for a third site. Becker offered career-oriented courses with some liberal arts courses.[45] Becker expressed an interest in Nasson in October 1984,

---

38   "USM to Lease Space?" *Sanford News*, July 24, 1984.

39   Ged Carbone, "USM Feels Pressure Over Nasson," *Journal Tribune*, August 2, 1984.

40   Nasson College, *Welcome*, 14; "Town Protecting Nasson Interest," *Sanford News*, August 21, 1984.

41   John Young, "Nasson Bankruptcy Auction Won't Be Postponed: Lawyer," *York County Coast Star*, October 24, 1984.

42   Nasson College, *Welcome*, 15.

43   See also, "Sale of Nasson Flatly Denied," *Sanford News*, September 25, 1984.

44   According to the 1981 College Blue Book, published by McMillan Company in New York, Becker was established in 1887 and became a private, coeducational four-year college. It specialized in business, secretarial skills, health, and retailing. Lee Burnett, "Mass. College Eyes Nasson Campus," *Journal Tribune*, October 2, 1984.

45   Nasson College, *Welcome*, 14.

which gave it a month to pull together its information and decide if it was seriously interested in buying Nasson. If, indeed, Becker was serious, and if it needed help from the town to buy in, it would have to move quickly to prepare an emergency article for the November 1984 town-meeting.

Negotiations between Becker and town officials followed. The basis for the plan was similar in some respects to the old TDC proposals. However, unlike TDC, Becker did not need federal assistance.[46] Becker's goal was to gradually restore the campus to its former four-year status, with the Massachusetts branches serving as a source of students.

Selectmen, the warrant committee, and other town officials strongly recommended assisting Becker in its purchase of Nasson. This would work by having the town acquire the library and the 136-acre Russell Environmental Studies Tract for $400,000. A sum of $250,000 was to be transferred from the town's $2.64 million in unappropriated "surplus funds," payable to Nasson at Becker's closing of the deal. The balance would be due one year after the closing date, with the source of funds to be determined by the November 1985 town-meeting.

Details included the following: Becker would lease the library and its contents from the town for not less than $20,000 a year for the first twenty years; Sanford High School students would be admitted to the college on an advanced placement basis; there would be shared use of facilities, such as the gym, the dining commons, and Shaw Field.[47] Becker would assume nearly $2 million in mortgages and other debts against Nasson. Total expenses to put the campus back into operation would be about $3 million.[48]

On October 19, selectmen approved the proposal. In response, Becker President Lloyd Van Buskirk confirmed acceptance of the plan. The warrant committee approved the plan on October 25, by a vote of 17 to 0.[49] Still, both Van Buskirk and Sanford's town manager acknowledged that final approval was required from the creditors and the bankruptcy court. Van Buskirk said that, if the plan was approved, the first freshman class could enter the fall of 1985. Becker officials were optimistic.[50]

Optimism was fleeting. The creditors' committee jumped in with an

46 Burnett, "Mass. College Eyes."
47 C. Scott Hoar, "Nasson Deal Coming Together," *Portland Press Herald*, October 20, 1984.
48 Young, "Nasson Bankruptcy Auction."
49 Linc Bedrosian, "Becker Plan Gets Unanimous 'Yes'," *Sanford News*, October 30, 1984.
50 Ged Carbone, "Sanford Officials, Becker Agree on Nasson," *Journal Tribune*, October 20, 1984.

announcement to correct what it said was a "misunderstanding"—the committee had no intention of postponing the auction, now scheduled for December.[51] The committee said that the offer from Becker was too speculative to justify delaying the auction.

As the next court date approached, the former Ricker College briefly entered the picture.[52] Bernard Maher was a former trustee of Ricker, and he wanted to testify before the bankruptcy court about the devastating effects that the foreclosure auction of Ricker's former campus had on the college's estate.[53] While Sanford and Nasson were going to split Maher's $500 witness fee, the creditors objected, arguing that his testimony would be totally irrelevant to Nasson's case. They said his appearance would just waste time and money. Fredrick Johnson, the bankruptcy court judge, agreed with the creditors. Maher would not be allowed testify.

Van Buskirk said that the creditors' committee kept pushing for more, and Becker College just did not have enough time to put the entire package together. In the end, they were just $100,000 to $200,000 short, which was still a lot of money under those conditions. That, along with the short time frames, made all the negotiations rushed and under pressure.[54] Further, Becker was going to have to spend perhaps a million dollars just to make repairs to some of the buildings and for startup costs.[55] Other unresolved questions persisted. For example, would Becker have degree-granting authority? Would the school be eligible to receive the trust fund? (Exactly which trust fund Van Buskirk was referring to is not clear.) And Nasson still owed $1 million in mortgages to the federal government.[56] With the property soon going to auction, Van Buskirk said he did not expect that Becker would be a bidder. He said it would be too difficult to reactivate the college after an auction. However, he did express his appreciation to the town for all its efforts to make the idea possible. Town Manager David Miller refused to give up on the campus, saying the town was still looking for a solution. He said that until the auction was held, they still had a chance.[57]

---

51   Lee Burnett, "Creditors Raise Specter of Auction," *Journal Tribune*, October 23, 1984.

52   Ricker College, located in Houlton, Maine, closed in 1978

53   "Maher's Testimony 'Irrelevant' to Nasson," *Journal Tribune*, November 7, 1984.

54   Jed Carbone, "Barring a 'Miracle,' Becker Out," *Journal Tribune*, November 12, 1984.

55   "Becker Won't Be at Nasson Auction," *Sanford News*, November 13, 1984.

56   Ibid.

57   C. Scott Hoar, "Judge: Nasson to Be Auctioned," *Portland Press Herald*, November 10, 1984.

When the hearing was finally held on November 9, 1984, Judge Johnson ruled that the auction would not be postponed.[58] The plan was confirmed by the bankruptcy court on November 9, 1984, and by the district court on November 16, 1984.[59]

Some people were bitter about the way things had played out. Miller said that Becker was to blame for the deal having fallen through.[60] He said the bankruptcy judge "would have bent over backwards" for Becker. All Becker had to say was "We're interested," but no one from Becker ever said those words. Miller did acknowledge that it was a complex deal and would have required several months to work out all the details. But, he said, Becker did not even try to buy the time it needed. On the other hand, in contrast to Becker's claim that the creditors kept asking for more, Hillman, the creditors' attorney, said that Becker kept offering less.[61] For his part, Judge Johnson said no one was to blame. He noted that the case had been in court for two years, and the parties were just not able to come to terms.

Miller reflected on one lost opportunity. Some months before, the town had entertained the idea of leasing the campus for about a year, in an effort to have more time to market it. Now, time was what everyone needed.

Exactly what might become of the campus? This was the great unknown. Town officials expected the contents of the buildings to sell first. The land and buildings would be harder to sell. The town knew the public was interested in the future use of the campus, which would determine the character of downtown Springvale for decades to come.[62] The upper campus was zoned for single-family residential use, so any proposal by a buyer to convert the dormitories to multifamily residences would require review by town agencies. However, the main campus was zoned for general residential use, which would allow apartments and some business development.

Becker seemed to be the last chance to avoid auction. The court refused to delay the auction any further and set December 10, 1984, as the date Nasson College was to be auctioned off.[63]

---

58 Hoar, "Judge."
59 *NEASC*, 80 B.R. at 602.
60 Linc Bedrosian, "Work Begins for Nasson Sale; 'No One to Blame'," *Sanford News*, November 20, 1984.
61 Ibid.
62 Editorial, "Sanford's Job Now That Becker's Out," *Journal Tribune*, November 14, 1984.
63 Nasson College, *Welcome*, 14.

THE FIRST AUCTION: 1984

The creditors' committee hired the Joseph Finn Co. Inc. of Boston. There were many details to address before the auction on December 10. Finn worked closely with James McLaughlin, former dean of students and now closing officer. Finn's staff sorted, arranged, and counted the equipment to be sold. It was all tagged. In the Lion's Den coffee shop, there were booths with tables, red swivel stools, a grill, soda fountain, fryolator, exhaust hood, and a menu board that still carried the final farewell from a student when the school closed; "GOOD-BYE, CAMP NASSON. IT'S BEEN REAL FUN. MISS YA."[64] In the Science Center, skeletons and fossils were up for grabs, and there was even a pickup truck to be sold. The gym could be sold as is, or the maple flooring could be ripped up and sold by itself, along with the bleachers and electric scoreboard. The chapel was marked, as was everything in the kitchen and dining hall. It was all tagged and inventoried.

Finn prepared advertising brochures and sent them out nationally to colleges and educational institutions. Finn had the real estate surveyed so that it could be offered as individual lots. The campus would be auctioned off in its entirety or by the lot, whichever brought more money for the creditors.[65] Finn explained that someone might want to purchase the president's house, and a prospective buyer could bid on just that, or he or she could bid on numerous individual properties.

Never say die. The town-meeting finally approved an article making $400,000 available to Becker, should the school actually show up at the auction and bid. While Becker had said it was no longer interested, at least the town was prepared if someone from Becker did show up.[66]

In response, Van Buskirk said, "I just don't understand it. I thought I made it pretty clear that we're not interested. Sooner or later you have to face reality."[67]

The plan was that, during the first day of the auction, bids for real estate would be considered, followed by a piecemeal lot sale of the gymnasium, the Little Theatre, the kitchen and dining commons, the bookstore, the library, the arts center, and Brown Hall.

The second day would see the Science Center equipment, Alumni Hall

---

64 Ged Carbone, "On the Block: It's Auctioneers' Turn at Nasson," *Journal Tribune*, November 20, 1984.
65 Bedrosian, "Work Begins."
66 Ged Carbone, "$400,000 Won't Sway Becker," *Journal Tribune*, November 21, 1984.
67 Ibid.

furnishings, and Reed Hall's kitchen equipment and furnishings sold off. Also, the Marland Hall kitchen equipment and lounge furnishings and the Allen Hall dormitory furniture would be sold. The third day would move the buildings and grounds equipment. The dormitory buildings, Prior-Hussey, Fobes Hall, Arts and Crafts, Hanscom Hall, and Folsom Halls I and II, along with the infirmary, would be sold. Finally, all the main and upper campus properties, the Russell Environmental Studies Tract, and Holdsworth Park would be sold.[68]

Even while all this preparation was going on, the town was still trying to find some way to reopen Nasson. In early December, TDC reentered the picture. It had a proposal that Dictar Associates would buy the campus and then lease the main campus to TDC. But in order for this plan to come to fruition, Dictar needed a guaranteed tenant, and TDC needed a guarantee from the state that it (TDC) would receive $1.5 million in state funding.[69] However, Bob Borgeault, executive director of the Bureau of Employment Training for the state, said that less than $900,000 was available for job-training programs in York County, and even that was already committed. Thus, the Dictar-TDC idea was just about impossible. Moreover, TDC would require a guarantee of $1.5 million a year for five years, which could not be done.[70]

Still, in the week before the auction, town selectmen met twice in executive session to try to find some way to save Nasson. But time was running out.

On December 10 and 11, a public inspection was offered for those looking to buy equipment. The auction itself was now scheduled for December 12, 13, and 14, 1984. On the first day of the inspection, between a hundred and two hundred college officials, businesspeople, and members of the public gathered at the college to examine the goods being offered in the liquidation. People strolled through the library looking at the twenty-five-page list of auction-able items, complete with numbers and accompanying descriptions. Various universities sent representatives to the library, assessing whether it contained anything there they wanted. Some browsed through the library's 130,000 books; others perused at dormitory furnishings. Prospective bidders went to registration tables set up in the library and were given packets of information about the college and the items available for bid.

---

68 Nasson College, *Welcome*, 15.

69 Ged Carbone, "TDC-Nasson Deal Called 'Impossible,'" *Journal Tribune*, November 29, 1984.

70 C. Scott Hoar, "Firm Revives Pitch for Nasson," *Portland Press Herald*, November 29, 1984.

All the publicity efforts by the auctioneer and others were reaching would-be buyers. Columbia College, a Chicago-based public and performing arts school, was interested in the library and science equipment.[71] Several dealers who were in the business of buying and selling property and equipment took an interest in the pending auction.

And in Worcester, Massachusetts, the head of a local college took notice of neighboring Becker College's interest. Once he found out that Becker was no longer interested, he went to Springvale to check out Nasson and to see if the school had any equipment he could use for his own school.[72] He tried to negotiate directly with the creditors' committee, but the committee just told him to show up at the auction. Over the next few days, he gave further thought to the idea of buying the whole campus and put out some feelers.

There were some behind-the-scenes meetings under way. Town officials did not say a word. The town administrator said he was not talking, at the request of the creditors' committee; according to the committee, any extra publicity would only confuse people.[73]

---

71 Richard Buhr, "Auction Day. Nasson: Going, Going, Almost Gone," *Journal Tribune*, December 13, 1984.

72 "Mattar Explains Purchase of Nasson Campus," *Sanford News*, December 24, 1984.

73 Nasson College, *Welcome*, 15.

NASSON COLLEGE IS SAVED

THE STORY BROKE ON the morning of December 12, 1984. At a meeting in the town hall conference room, Stephen Morris announced that Edward Paul Mattar III, president of Central New England College in Worcester, Massachusetts, had come forward and taken an option on the core campus.[74] He'd paid about $327,000 in cash for Brown Hall, Alumni Hall, and the MSAC (the gym and dining commons). For the three other buildings (the Science Center and the Marland Hall and Allen Hall dormitories), he'd negotiated with the federal government to assume $973,664 in education mortgages. He'd also paid $5,000 to the trustees of the George Nasson estate; $50,000 to Katherine Hildreth; and $25,000 in severance claims, for a total "payment" by Mattar of $1,380,664.

Why did Mattar succeed where so many others had failed? The big difference between Mattar's plan and all the others was that Mattar put down a cash deposit, which no one else could do, according to Hillman, the creditors' attorney.[75] A big component of that was that Mattar needed no third-party money, no UDAG grants, no job-training funds, and no guaranteed tenants. As a result, everyone he needed to talk to was able to assemble in one room; it would not take months to make a deal.[76] Also, since he recognized he did not need the entire campus—no need to obtain the upper campus dorms, Pryor-Hussey or Folsom—those properties could

---

74 Ibid.
75 C. Scott Hoar, "Bay State Group Agrees to Buy Nasson College," *Portland Press Herald*, December 12, 1984; C. Scott Hoar, "Nasson Backer Explains Plans for Reorganization," *Portland Press Herald*, December 21, 1984.
76 "Mattar Explains Purchase."

be auctioned off and provide additional money for the creditors.[77] Mattar also made it clear that Nasson was not unique. He said there were other schools that had closed, so he could take his business elsewhere.[78] In addition, the creditors and everyone else recognized that this really was the last chance to preserve any hope of reopening a college there.[79] And, of course, the creditors knew no guarantee could be made when it came to who would actually show up to bid or what they might receive if everything went to auction. Also playing into Mattar's success was the eagerness of just about everyone to see him succeed. Certainly, Mattar was seen as the last hope of any chance of saving or resurrecting the college. A thorough check into his background might have made some people pause, because his background in saving Central New England College was not quite the great success it appeared to be.[80] Certain character traits in his past would come to haunt Nasson.[81]

Town officials revealed that they and Mattar had been meeting for sixteen days of negotiations and executive-session meetings. Nasson College would reopen. The rest of the auction was canceled midafternoon on December 12.[82] The plan was that the college would reopen as a two-and four-year nonresidential school geared toward computer science.[83] Or it would include residential students living in Marland and Allen Halls. Mattar said that by September 1986, he expected to have those dorms filled.[84]

---

77   The properties that were sold brought in about $500,000. C. Scott Hoar, "Nasson Receives $500,000 from Auction of Buildings," *Portland Press Herald*, December 13, 1984.

78   Mattar was right about that. For an oversight of closed colleges, visit www. closedcolleges.org.

79   "Mattar Explains Purchase."

80   In the late 1970s, Worcester Junior College was heavily in debt. Mattar was brought in as a management consultant to help close the school. Instead, within a year he became president of the college, even though he had no experience in education. Rather than closing the school, he renamed it and seemed to turn it around. He received much praise for his efforts. Still, early on, he was ordered by the Massachusetts Board of Higher Education to stop awarding bachelor's degrees to students who graduated from what was still Worcester Junior College.

81   At the same time as he ran CNEC, Mattar operated several unrelated businesses. For example, he owned the Feel Fit Health Center. In 1984, it suddenly closed, and he refused to refund any membership fees or pay his rent, which was said to amount to more than $26,000

82   See also Michael Kranish, "Sale Arranged for Maine's Bankrupt Nasson College," *The Boston Globe*, December 12, 1984.

83   Ibid.

84   Richard Buhr, "Nasson: Live-In, Off-Campus," *Journal Tribune*, January 15,

Dictar Associates, which had tried to make a deal with TDC, bought Pryor-Hussey for $27,500 and New Division / Upper Campus I / Fobes Hall for $52,500. The president's house, with Reed Hall attached, sold for $60,000.[85] International House, next to Pryor-Hussey, sold for $52,000.[86] These properties, now that they were in private hands, would incur property taxes; Nasson had never had to pay property taxes. That pleased the town. Also sold were the buildings and grounds facility on Mill Street, the Seminar Building and the Bradford Block, the Home Management House, New Division II / Upper Campus II / Hanscom Hall, Grove Hall, and the 125-acre Russell Environmental Studies Tract (Deering Pond). Other properties sold included Holmes Hall, Beaver Hill and the Hilltop House, Ridley House, and an old garage at the corner of Mill and Main streets.[87]

The total funds received from the sale of assets and from other claims exceeded $919,606. Of this amount, $559,418 was paid to appraisers, consultants, surveyors, lawyers and liquidators, leaving $360,188 for unsecured creditors.

Mattar's proposal was a complicated one. The purchase was contingent on the town appropriating $550,000 to buy the library and the 130,000 volumes in the library, which would be leased back to Nasson for $1 a year. Also, the town would take over the $130,000 debt on the library.

The agreement was also conditional upon Mattar's receipt from the state of Maine (or the appropriate agency thereof) written assurances that Nasson's charter and degree-granting authority remained in full force and effect or a final order of the bankruptcy court that such charter and degree-granting authority had not been revoked and that Nasson's board of trustees remained duly constituted.[88]

But first things first. The town-meeting members had to approve the town's participation at the January 29, 1985, special town-meeting. Selectmen endorsed the proposal, wherein the $550,000 for the purchase of the library would be transferred from unappropriated funds. Negotiations were held with the Department of Education to cut the $130,000 debt on the library, and the department indicated it would do so.

This time, the town-meeting members went along with the deal, voting 79 to 31 to approve it. As part of the agreement, in lieu of taxes,

1985.

85   Buhr, "Auction Day."

86   Hoar, ""Nasson Receives $500,000."

87   C. Scott Hoar, "Committee Discusses Nasson Deal Conditions," *Portland Press Herald*, January 17, 1985.

88   *Nasson College v. NEASC*, 80 B.R. 600, 603 (1988).

the college would make payments of not less than $10,000 a year to the town, beginning with the sixth year of the lease, if economic conditions allowed it. Nasson would also have the option to purchase the building back from the town.[89]

There was more. The Department of Education and the Department of Justice[90] agreed to reduce the nearly $1 million debt on four campus buildings to create a net present value savings of 20 percent, and there would be a short moratorium on the payments by the college (in other words, Mattar).[91] Another agreement had to be made between the college and the creditors. The government would reduce the debt only if the college could negotiate with the creditors' committee to have the government released from Section 506 claims concerning the actual expenses of maintaining, operating, and guarding the estate over the previous year and a half, plus appropriate shares of the legal fees involved. That all came to $170,000 for the maintenance and legal fees of $230,000. The creditors were to receive $120,000 to $130,000 of cash belonging to Nasson College in unrestricted endowments.[92] Mattar was to continue to pay off the $1 million mortgage debt (now reduced) owed to the federal government.[93]

And there was even more. On February 12, 1984, a hearing was conducted by the bankruptcy court on the joint motion of the creditors' committee and Mattar, "Regarding Consummation of Second Amended Plan of Reorganization." An order dated March 8, 1985, was prepared for the court's approval. That order contained the following language:

> That the Debtor [Nasson College] has maintained continuous operations since the petition date, and the Debtor may continue all operations as a college with full

89 Nasson College, *Welcome*, 16. It's not clear who actually "owned" the buildings at this point. The US Department of Education held mortgages on some of the buildings, and presumably, titles to those properties were held by Nasson College, which would have made the college part of the bankruptcy estate. It is not clear that the town was to own any other building besides the library.

90 The Department of Justice was involved because the Department of Education was legally barred from adding to the federal debt, so any negotiations that would have that effect would have to be approved by the Justice Department. John Young, "Nasson College Recovery Plan Authorized by Sanford Voters," *York County Coast Star*, January 30, 1985.

91 Richard Buhr, "Last Major Hurdle Overcome in Deal to Reopen Nasson," *Journal Tribune*, February 12, 1985.

92 Various press reports gave varying amounts, and other reports contribute to the conflicting assignments of exactly which buildings were sold to whom and when and in what sequence.

93 Nasson College, *Welcome*, 16.

degree-granting authority, powers, licenses, privileges, and accreditations in and to the same extent as it enjoyed as of the date of the petition, November 4, 1982.[94]

As the saying goes, mistakes were made.

It turned out that the court was not aware of the termination of Nasson's accreditation by the New England Association of Schools and Colleges (NEASC) as of May 1, 1983. Moreover, the court was not fully cognizant of the significance of accreditation. In fact, not once during the February 12 meeting was accreditation even mentioned. Thus, at the time of the March 8 order, neither the court nor Mattar was aware of any accreditation problem. Evidently, while Mattar was concerned about accreditation, no one bothered to pick up the phone and call NEASC.

In any event, the rest of the plans all managed to come together. There were many documents to be signed and details to work out. But by the end of March 1985, the bankruptcy court in Portland had approved the reconstitution plan. In the end, the multiparty negotiations were all successful. Nasson College would reopen.[95]

Next, the Nasson College trustees—yes, the old college was still technically in existence all this time—met to ratify the action of Board Chairman Stephen Morris, who had signed the December 10, 1984, agreement to sell the four core buildings to Mattar.[96] Morris was also authorized to execute all necessary transactions needed to effect the final closing.[97] Mattar signed the settlement agreements with the US

---

94 *NEASC*, 80 B.R. at 603

95 Nasson College, *Welcome*, 16.

96 The "four core buildings" included Brown Hall, Alumni Hall, and the Memorial Student Activity Center, which usually included the dining commons. If the dining commons was not the fourth building, it's not clear what was. The Science Center, Marland Hall, and Allen Hall were all part of the federal mortgages, and the town had already purchased the library. What never seemed to be clear was exactly who held the title to the properties after Mattar's payments. Some reports suggest that Mattar personally bought them; other reports suggest he paid the creditors' committee directly for the school's debts. Or perhaps he gave his money directly to the college, which then used it to pay its debts. This makes the most sense, as one generally can't just "buy" a not-for-profit college. Mattar agreed. When he purchased the core campus in 1984, he pointed out that the college was not sold to him. "It can't be sold, and nobody's buying it. The Nasson trustees are going to re-open the college." "Mattar Explains Purchase of Nasson Campus," *Sanford News*, December 24, 1984.

The distinction was eventually to become very important. One thing is certain; Mattar personally did not assume any of Nasson's debts.

97 C. Scott Hoar, "Meetings Herald Nasson Rebirth," *Portland Press Herald*, March

Department of Education in his official capacity as an officer of Nasson College. He did not personally borrow funds from the department; nor did he personally assume the debts of Nasson College.[98]

With the physical plant transferred, next came the transfer of power. Part of the deal was that Mattar's appointees would replace all the legacy trustees of the college. Old members of the board of trustees resigned, and new members, all selected by Mattar, were elected. None of them was local to the Sanford area. Chairman Stephen Morris and Treasurer H. Allen Mapes also resigned, and Mattar was named the new chairman of the board.[99]

On March 20, 1985, Nasson College was released from oversight of the bankruptcy court. At last, the creditors were no longer in control of the college.[100]

In the following weeks, administrative staff was named. Barbara Holt became the new administrative coordinator. Her assignment was to organize and coordinate daily administrative affairs and to work with the new business manager, Margaret Sevigny and Dean of Students James J. McLaughlin, who were the only carryovers from old Nasson. Sevigny had been the Nasson's controller before it closed. McLaughlin was Dean of Students.

Academically, Mattar planned to implement a program similar to the program he imposed on Central New England College. When Mattar took over CNEC in 1978, it had 375 students and the school was experiencing financial problems. Seven years later, CNEC claimed to have 2,200 students and a new $8 million campus in Westborough, Massachusetts.[101]

Mattar's idea was that the school had to be different to distinguish it from the competition. Rather than offering yet another liberal arts program, along with hundreds of other colleges around the country, Nasson would offer courses that Mattar believed were needed and wanted in southern Maine but were not offered anywhere else. Some liberal arts

---

14, 1985.

98 US Dept. of Education, "Report to the Inspector General," May 7, 1998.

99 Nasson College, *Welcome*, 18.

100 C. Scott Hoar, "Nasson Begins New Life under Mattar," *Portland Press Herald*, March 21, 1985.

101 Nasson College, *Welcome*, 7. But it was apparently all an illusion. A 1987 audit of Central New England College revealed that the school was $14 million in debt. Mattar was forced to resign in 1988, and in 1989 the college closed. In 1991, a Massachusetts Bank sued Mattar, claiming he had personally defaulted on three loans. The bank foreclosed on his 5,500-square-foot home in Worcester, Massachusetts. ("Boulder Bank Owner Leaves Ugly Trail," *Sanford News*, September 3, 1998 [citing an article by Al Lewis, *Rocky Mountain News*].)

classes would still be offered, but they were there to help students learn to think, reason, and maintain a sense of ethics and values. Overall, the goal was to be different, distinguished, and cost-effective.[102] Rather than offer a typical thirty-hour course meeting three days a week for an hour or two each session, weekend college students would attend two three-hour classes each week. They would have the same amount of class time, but it would be scheduled around work hours.

On a beautiful summer evening in July 1985, there was a grand celebration. The invitation read:

Nasson College

Sanford / Springvale, Maine

invites you to celebrate the

reopening of the College on Saturday, July 13, 1985

on the Nasson College campus

Town selectmen, warrant committee members, and planning board members joined Nasson College officials at the campus flagpole for a dedication ceremony to celebrate Nasson's rebirth. Mattar saluted Town Administrator David Miller for his efforts on behalf of Nasson's reconstitution. Guests were taken on a tour of Marland Hall, which was undergoing renovations to its dormitory rooms. Attendees enjoyed presentations by the Sanford Maine Stage Company in the Little Theatre, guided tours, a reception in Reed Hall,[103] and performances by the St. Louis Boys Choir of Paris, France, in the Gallery Room of the Anderson Learning Center.

The new Nasson trustees announced a number of innovative academic programs, which were designed to lead to a master of business administration degree (MBA), a bachelor of science degree (BS) in business administration and management, or an associate in science degree in management. Nasson College would also provide shorter diploma and certificate programs in a variety of areas, such as word processing, computer applications, supervisory skills, and principles of accounting and bookkeeping.[104] Plans also included a master of science degree in health administration. According to Mattar, the MS in health administration would be a one-year program for health professionals. This was designed for the preparation of hospital administrators and health-care administrators and planners, as well as for career advancement

---

102 Nasson College, *Welcome*, 7.
103 Nasson College, *Welcome*, 7. At that point, the college did not own Reed Hall.
104 Ibid, 18.

in health maintenance organizations, mental-health agencies, home-health agencies, and health-planning agencies. The entire program was designed to be completed in just fifty-four Saturdays of full-time class work.[105] Some programs offered by the new school were described as "fully creditable towards associate and bachelor's degrees."[106]

It's not clear exactly what that meant.

In fact, most of the academic programs offered by the new Nasson College could be completed in just twenty-one weeks for day students, or twenty-eight weeks for evening students. Some programs would take up to thirty-five weeks for night students. The idea was to offer classes convenient for students. Students could take classes in the morning and have the rest of the day to work. With an eye toward the failing industries in the area, programs were designed to meet the training needs of men and women who had been displaced by closing factories. Such displaced workers could receive tuition grants of up to $4,800 provided through the Trade Readjustment Act.[107]

Frank Mazzaglia was appointed dean of business programs. He had a BS from Boston College, a master's in education from Boston State College, and an MBA from Suffolk University. He was, at that time, in the process of completing a doctoral program at Harvard University. Previously, he had been chairman of the master of business administration and executive programs at Anna Maria College in central Massachusetts.

William Perry was named Nasson's interim president. Perry had been vice president and dean of the graduate school of Lesley College in Cambridge, Massachusetts, and was a founding president of Corning Community College in Corning, New York, for nine years. Most recently, he had been education consultant to the Kingdom of Lesotho, in southern Africa.[108]

The school renovated some of the campus buildings. Administrative offices were in the Anderson Learning Center. (Brown Hall, the old administration building, was not used for the school at that time.) In the beginning, the ALC was the entire campus, and contained the library, a computer laboratory, and classrooms. Leaks in the roof were fixed, ceiling tiles were replaced, and new coats of paint were applied. Offices were rearranged, and classrooms were created in the basement, which previously had been used primarily for storage.

Classes began on July 12, 1985, with an enrollment of sixty students,

---

105 Ibid, 3.
106 Ibid.
107 Ibid.
108 Ibid, 5.

ten more than the number expected. Once the regular school year got underway, enrollment was projected to be 150 students.[109]

Optimism was in the air.

> In fact, everyone at Nasson from the maintenance crew to the secretaries and receptionists up to the administrative personnel always seem to be busy; there is much to do to make Nasson a success once again. The college appears to be heading in the right direction, and those walking into the Anderson Learning Center recently notice that the level of excitement has picked up even more. It makes quite a difference when people are working, professors are teaching and students are attending classes again. The college is alive again with the sounds of a healthy college, a sound that has been missing for far too long. The residents of Sanford-Springvale are glad those sounds and Nasson College are back again.[110]

The college produced a catalog, of a sort. It was four pages on newsprint, but it was something. Besides announcing the various classes and programs (such as the Weekend College, and the Accelerated Saturday MBA), the school announced that up to 50 percent introductory scholarships were "available now." The school advertised $50,000 in scholarship assistance on a first-come, first-served basis through Nasson's board of trustees "in appreciation for the loyalty of Sanford-Springvale residents and [Nasson's] area friends."[111] Tuition rates were $90 per credit for part-time undergraduate courses, $120 per credit for the Weekend College, and $200 per credit for graduate programs. All these figures reflected the 50 percent scholarship discounts.[112] Supposedly, these rates were the same as at the 1982 levels.[113]

In order to qualify for admission to Nasson College, prospective students had to fill out a form in the four-page catalog, identify the courses they wanted to take, and include payment. Neither high school or other academic achievement was mentioned as being a requirement for admission

---

109 Ibid, 3.
110 Ibid, 20.
111 Nasson College catalog, Summer 1985.
112 Ibid, 4.
113 Ibid, 4. Actually, they were a little bit cheaper. For the 1982–83 school year, a full-time student at Nasson College paid $5,195 for tuition and fees. At twelve credits per semester, or twenty-four for the year, that comes to about $216 per credit hour. (Nasson College catalog, 1982, 27.)

to the college. The catalog showed the original Nasson College seal, still carrying the 1935 date. (Nasson Institute opened in 1912. In 1935, it officially became a college.)

The fall catalog was larger, eight pages, although the scholarship funds were now down to $30,000. In addition to the complete lineup of courses described above, there were other innovations. Students could now take courses by video. "[Each course,] successfully completed, is worth three college credits,"[114] but the catalog didn't explain what that really meant. Video courses included "Exploring Language: Thinking, Writing, Communications," "The Religious Quest," and "Time's Harvest: Exploring the Future." The catalog said that "overnight accommodations [were] available,"[115] but no details were provided. Tuition costs were less for Sanford-Springvale residents than for nonresidents and were generally less costly than they'd been during the previous summer program.[116]

WHAT MIGHT HAVE BEEN AND WHAT WAS

Mattar's plans were for the sort of educational program described above. Everyone else envisioned a campus alive with full-time boarding students sleeping in the dorms and taking meals in the cafeteria, attending sporting events, and clubs and arts organizations hosting educational and entertaining events. But that kind of college program never quite emerged.[117]

And yet at one point, that kind of program was actually considered, at least in part, at least by someone. A draft of a regular college catalog was produced for the 1985–87 period. This seventy-four-page document seemed to pick up where the 1982 Nasson catalog had left off. In fact, it identified itself as volume XXXVIII. (The 1982 catalog was the XXXVII edition.) In the section on the history of the college, the current program was described: "In 1985, in a remarkable resurgence, Nasson College was released from the control of the bankruptcy court and had all of its previous powers, rights, authority, licenses, and privileges restored by order of the Federal Courts. In July of 1985, students were admitted to new Master Degree Programs and excitingly relevant and timely undergraduate programs." Undergraduate classes were to be twelve weeks long, and classes

---

114 Nasson College catalog, Fall 1985, 3.

115 Ibid, 3.

116 Ibid, 8.

117 The community can't say it wasn't warned. As early as December 1984, Mattar explained that Nasson would not be a liberal arts college in the sense it was before. "Mattar Explains Purchase."

were only given from 8:00 a.m. to 10:55 a.m. and 6:00 p.m. to 9:55 p.m. The school still recognized the liberal arts. "All degree students will participate in the mind-stretching which results from intensive study of the great works of literature, the arts and the social sciences. Success in management requires the ability to think, reason and communicate effectively, as well as a philosophical grounding in ethics and values."[118] Required courses for a bachelor's degree included, among various business classes, English composition, philosophy (ethics), American history, fine arts, and more. The course description for comparative government was taken almost word-for-word from the 1982–83 catalog.

Whoever was drafting the catalog copied a little too closely. The catalog boasted, "Nasson College is a 10.4 acre campus which includes four dormitories (Marland Hall, Allen Hall, Folsom I & II), athletic facilities, classrooms, offices, computer lab, Shaw Playing Field, Holdsworth Lakeside Park, Little Theatre, etc."[119] In fact, after the reopening, Shaw Field and Holdsworth Park were no longer part of the school.

The draft catalog envisioned academic recognitions as well. These included a Dean's List; George Nasson Scholars; and the Bertha C. Miltmore Alumni Award, given each year to a freshman or sophomore student. Scholarships were available too, such as the Mary Lord Bailey, the Grossman, the Saul Shalit Memorial Scholarship Fund, and others, right out of the 1982 catalog. Was there really money set aside for these awards? It seemed unlikely, given everything else that described the new school. Full-time students were to pay $2,600 per term, almost exactly the same as the tuition during the final year of old Nasson.

So what happened to all this? Someone obviously did a lot of work, basically designing a whole new college. One can only speculate. Most likely, this expansive organization may have been what the town and the Nasson community wanted, but it was not what Mattar wanted. The draft catalog never saw the light of day.

Nevertheless, the fact was that this was not a reopening of Nasson College as it had been. In spite of the catalog drafter's expectations, few resident students, no real resident dormitories, no dining commons, no student clubs, no sports teams, and no use of the gym at all existed. And little or no effort was made to connect to the still existing, if somewhat dormant, Nasson College Alumni Association. And one big thing was missing from the printed catalogs—a clear statement of accreditation.

Still, 157 students enrolled for the fall of 1985, and by the end of the

---

118 From the draft college catalog for 1985-87.
119 Ibid.

year, twelve students were reported to be living in Marland Hall, while that building was being renovated.[120]

OTHER CAMPUS BUILDINGS FIND NEW LIFE

Other parts of the campus were put to use. The Little Theatre at Nasson became home to the Maine Stage Company of Sanford. Maine Stage declared "We've moved!" and promoted its 1985 summer season. Five shows, running from June to September, included *Sleuth*, *H.M.S. Pinafore*, *Godspell*, *Stop the World – I Want to Get Off*, *I Ought to Be in Pictures*, and *Jonathan Livingston Seagull*. The company also had a children's theater program on Saturday mornings.[121] The theater group had been performing in the Sanford Town Hall Auditorium, but the arrangement was not very satisfactory to either the group or the town. The company painted and restored the exterior of the theater and planned to extend the stage. Mattar said that, while he would not charge the group rent to use the space, they would have to pay for utilities.[122]

THE ALUMNI ASSOCIATION HANGS ON

Throughout this period, the Nasson College Alumni Association never missed a beat. Year in and year out, as far back as the fall of 1983, alumni held homecoming. Often, the event was not held on campus but at other locations, such as the Unicorn and Lion in Kennebunk, Smiths' Red Apple Farm, the Sanford Golf Club, and Spectators Sports Bar.

Fortunately, before the college filed for bankruptcy in 1982, someone had the foresight to separate the two organizations. Thus, the NCAA was not caught up in the bankruptcy and remained an independent corporation.

---

120 C. Scott Hoar, "Reborn Nasson Forges Ahead. Accreditation Status Not Yet Settled, However," *Portland Press Herald*, December 31, 1985. Information on housing in Marland Hall included the following: "Rooms are available for students in Nasson College's Marland Hall. All rooms have two twin beds, and each room shares a bath with an adjoining room. Students may share a room with another student or may have a room alone, although the baths are still shared. Linens will be provided. Public telephones are located on each hall. The rooms are not furnished with televisions. Food services are not available on campus, although restaurants are located close by. Open coil cooking is not permitted in the dormitory; microwave ovens are permitted."

121 Main Stage Company, "Join the Celebration," flyer, Summer 1985.

122 Richard Buhr, "Stage Company Will Hold Shows at Nasson Theater," *Journal Tribune*, March 26, 1985.

It had its own IRS employer identification number and separate bank accounts. It was never involved with any of the auctions and was never acquired by Mattar.

At the association's board meeting in October 1985, Dean McLaughlin, who was then back on the college's payroll, said that five people were living in Marland Hall, and the Lion's Den had been converted into the dining area. (When Marland Hall was constructed in 1957, the lower level served as the dining hall for the entire college. After the dining commons was built in 1962, that area of Marland Hall became the Lion's Den coffee shop.) Other information from Mattar's school said there would be no food services available.

McLaughlin expected the dorm to be filled to capacity for the spring semester of 1986. (It wasn't.) Current enrollment at the college was 137. Also at that meeting, alumni president Robert Stone announced that communications between the alumni association and the new school were finally under way and that Frank Mazzaglia, Nasson College business manager, would run a seminar to increase the effectiveness of fund-raising for both the college and the alumni association.

At the November 1985 meeting, Dean Mazzaglia spoke to the alumni. He said that many alumni were stopping in to see the college in operation and these alumni were ready to give their support to assist with the revival of Nasson College.[123] But at the meeting on February 8, 1986, President Stone said that, to date, he had been unable to schedule a meeting with Mattar.[124]

In February 1988, Stone reported that the association, which had given almost all of its funds to the college before the school closed, had been left $2,000 by Faye Everett Grace, Nasson Institute, class of 1926. However, before the association could receive the money, its lawyer had to prove to Grace's estate that the organization remained viable. Stone and the others were able to do so. With that bequest (minus the attorney's fees), the association had a balance of $2,796.68.[125] At the meeting on April 23, 1988, Stone reported that the college had offered free use of all campus facilities for homecoming 1988. Barbara Holt, the college administrator, would be the college's liaison to the association. Also, she agreed to give the

---

123 Frank Mazzaglia, "Minutes of the Nasson College Alumni Council," November 11, 1985.

124 Robert Stone, "Minutes of the Nasson College Alumni Council," February 8, 1986.

125 "Minutes of the Nasson College Alumni Council," February 27, 1988.

association the names of recent graduates who were interested in actively participating in the alumni association.[126]

Still, optimism among the alumni was sometimes hard to see. An announcement in the fall of 1988 was less than encouraging:

> We realize there hasn't been a homecoming in quite a long time. We feel we have all lost touch with our roots and it is about time we go home.
>
> This October 1, 1988, the Nasson College Alumni Association will sponsor Homecoming at Shaw Field. This may be the only homecoming for the next five years so we hope you all can attend.
>
> Nasson College has been supportive of this event but not financially. We are trying to sponsor this event on a shoestring. It is very difficult, at this point, to predict how much this is all going to cost. We are starting with close to nothing, but we feel with your financial support we can do it.
>
> For a small donation of $18.00 per person (more if you can afford it) we can get this homecoming off the ground. We would really like this to work so please show your support.
>
> PLEASE SEND MONEY BEFORE SEPTEMBER 26, 1988!

NASSON COLLEGE OPERATIONS

The new Nasson College graduated its first students in the summer of 1986. In the first graduation ceremony since the school closed in 1983, Academic Dean Dr. Lawrence Stahlberg and Barbara Holt awarded degrees in business administration and science and certificates in word processing and computer-based accounting. In his remarks, Mattar referred to "our seventy-fifth year of operations."[127] Receiving honorary degrees were Maine Governor Joseph Brennan and David Miller, former Sanford town administrator. Alumni President Robert Stone was on the dais with Mattar and the governor.

---

126 Ibid.
127 John Gold, "Nasson College Graduation Is New Beginning," *Journal Tribune*, July 28, 1986.

At least in its first years, the reconstituted Nasson College seemed to be a success. The first year, enrollment exceeded expectations, according to Mattar.[128] He had predicted that the school would have fifty full-time students enrolled in the accelerated MBA program and weekend courses and one hundred in the part-time program. As it turned out, the first year had seventy to seventy-six students in the full-time program and about seventy in the part-time program.

Mattar said that, even after he had operated the school for about a year, his full team was not yet in place. He thought the faculty was very good, and students' evaluations of teachers were positive. According to Mattar, the school's current president, Dr. William Perry, was only there on an interim basis until a permanent replacement could be found. (Of course, the old Nasson College suffered from the same lack of presidential stability in its last ten years or so.) Mattar acknowledged that upgrading Marland Hall was taking longer than he had expected. But he expected the work to be done by spring, housing fifty or sixty full-time dormitory students in the fall of 1986. Mattar claimed that he already had almost as many students as the old Nasson had had when it closed in 1983. (He didn't; old Nasson had had about 280 students at the end of its final year.) He also announced that the school would open a branch campus in Portland, Maine, for students who did not want to travel as far south as Springvale.

Mattar paid credit to the many people in the local area who were big supporters of Nasson. He noted that the business community was very cooperative, even those merchants who were never paid for debts owed by the old school. He also thanked Allen Mapes, head of Mapes Oil for his contributions, noting that Mapes had helped the college obtain reasonable prices for its heating oil needs. Overall, Mattar acknowledged "a whole lot of people who have gone that extra mile" for the school.

On a sad note, James J. McLaughlin, known as "Dean Mac" to a whole generation of students at Nasson, was finally let go by Mattar.[129] According

---

128 Linc Bedrosian, "Things Looking Good for Nasson after 3 Terms," *Sanford News*, January 21, 1986.

129 McLaughlin began work at Nasson College in 1958, working for President Roger Gay. His first assignment was to "get the school into shape" so it could join the National Collegiate Athletic Association. He later became dean of students and head of the behavioral sciences division. In his various roles, he oversaw athletics, took care of dormitory students, and conducted many other activities. Under Mattar, for a time, he helped organize alumni groups. Of note, Dean Mac was the school's caretaker between the time the school closed in 1983 and when Mattar took over in 1985. After leaving Nasson, McLaughlin landed on his feet. By 1989, he had become president of Unity College in Unity, Maine. Paul Dest, "What's New for James McLaughlin," *Sanford News*, November 7, 1989.

to Mattar, he had tried to find a good position for McLaughlin, but no job similar to that of dean of students existed at the new Nasson. He had offered suggestions, but McLaughlin, saying the available alternatives were not what he wanted or needed, resigned. McLaughlin's story was different; Mattar, he said, had simply laid him off, providing no explanation.[130]

THE ACCREDITATION PROBLEM

As some students noticed, all was not well. To know why, we have to revisit an old issue.

The original Nasson College was first accredited by the NEASC in 1960 and was still accredited at the time it filed its Chapter 11 bankruptcy petition in November 1982.[131] Shortly thereafter, NEASC's Commission on Institutions of Higher Education informed the school that the commission was concerned about the school's fiscal stability. NEASC "requested," which is to say ordered, Nasson to show cause in writing by January 21, 1983, why the commission should not recommend termination of its accreditation.[132] The record does not show whether Nasson actually complied with the request, but in any event, NEASC did not take any further action that winter. Nasson continued to offer educational programs until the end of the 1982–83 academic year, and the accreditation remained in effect until the end.

At the April 25, 1983, meeting of the college board of trustees, the board voted to cease operations as of graduation day, May 1, 1983. The NEASC Commission then met and voted to recommend to its executive committee that "the accreditation status of Nasson College as an educational institution be terminated effective May 2, 1983."[133] The commission made provisions for the protection of students nearing graduation. The school was officially notified of the commission's action by letter dated April 27, 1983. The letter explained, "Because only institutions offering instruction may be accredited, membership status will cease effective with the conclusion of educational activities."[134] The commission did tell Nasson that it had a right to appeal the decision.

Then, on May 10, 1983, after the school had graduated its last class, the executive committee of NEASC voted "that the accreditation of Nasson

---

130 Bedrosian, "Things Looking Good."
131 *NEASC*, 80 B.R. 600 (1988).
132 Ibid, 602.
133 *Id.*
134 *Id.*

College be terminated effective May 2, 1983, with the stipulation that accreditation will be maintained for degree-granting purposes for those students enrolled at Nasson in the Spring of 1983 with thirty-six (36) hours or less remaining to earn their Nasson degree."[135]

At the next meeting of Nasson's trustees on May 25, 1983, the trustees essentially agreed with NEASC. No appeal was made by Nasson; nor was the termination of accreditation brought to the bankruptcy court's attention by Nasson or the creditors' committee, which, at the time, was very zealous in protecting the estate's property.

When Nasson College reopened in 1985, its new officers and trustees attempted to resume the school's accreditation with NEASC. For its part, NEASC insisted that Nasson's accreditation ended in 1983 and that it now must apply for accreditation de novo and resubmit to the accreditation process.[136]

Nasson sued NEASC in the bankruptcy court. Nasson's argument was that accreditation was "property" of the estate and that, as such, NEASC had violated the automatic stay of Section 362(a) of the Bankruptcy Code by terminating Nasson's accreditation. In essence, the law states that all property an estate has at the time of a bankruptcy filing remains part of the estate. Thus, the question for the court was whether "accreditation," which was an educational *status*, was within the meaning of "property" under the law.[137]

According to NEASC's Commission on Institutions of Higher Learning, accreditation is a status granted to an educational institution that has been found to meet or exceed stated criteria of educational quality.[138] Thus, accreditation status, while valuable to the institution, is, in essence, held in the nature of a trust for the commission and the public and assures all that the institution has clearly defined objectives that meet criteria published by the commission. Importantly, the status is not permanent. An institution must continuously comply with the requirements for accreditation. Accreditation cannot be bought, sold, pledged, or exchanged; it may not be liquidated by a trustee in bankruptcy or distributed to creditors. Thus, the court concluded, accreditation is not property and, therefore, cannot be property of an estate.[139]

The court concluded that whatever the proper scope of judicial review

---

135 *Id.*
136 *Id.* 603.
137 *Id.* 604.
138 *Id.* citing NEASC's Accreditation Handbook, 1.
139 *Id.*

a court might have in monitoring associations such as NEASC, it does not include de novo review of its evaluative decisions.[140]

In response, Nasson argued that, in refusing to reinstate its accreditation, NEASC was in violation of the court's order of March 8, 1985. But the court found that that order, to the extent it seemed to continue Nasson's accreditation, was erroneous because the court was unaware that NEASC had already withdrawn Nasson's accreditation in May 1983. The court noted that accreditation was terminated because Nasson ceased educational operations, not because it filed for bankruptcy.[141]

Mattar's Nasson could not restore old Nasson's accreditation. However, once the lawsuit ended, Nasson moved forward with reaccreditation efforts. Louis D'Allesandro, president of Nasson at that time, said that he had contacted both NEASC and the Association of Independent Colleges and Schools, a national accrediting organization, to apply for accreditation.[142] In fact, it appears Nasson never reapplied to NEASC for new accreditation[143] and was never accredited by AICS.[144] Nevertheless, the school *was* accredited by the Accrediting Council for Continuing Education & Training up until 1994.[145]

NASSON COLLEGE: OPEN FOR BUSINESS

The school's lack of accreditation did not go unnoticed. Bob Lovegrove, a Nasson MBA graduate, said that, without accreditation, the degree did not mean very much.[146] Judith Morin, who received a certificate in computer-based accounting, said the school's lack of accreditation did bother her a lot, but she felt that the school was working hard to get it. Others also spoke well of the school. Peter Bowen said he worked hard for the MBA

---

140 *Id.* 605, citing *Marlboro Corp. v. Ass'n of Independent Colleges and Schools, Inc.*, 556 F.2d 78, 80, n. 2 (1st Cir. 1977).

141 *Id.* 606. Obviously. The college filed for bankruptcy on November 4, 1982, but accreditation was not withdrawn until the school closed on May 1, 1983, some six months after the bankruptcy filing.

142 C. Scott Hoar, "Nasson Begins Process to Regain Accreditation," *Portland Press Herald*, c. January 1988.

143 *Spring v. Trustees of the Hervey A. Hanscom Trust*, Mass. Probate and Family Court, Docket No. 93E-0080 (March 18, 1994) at 18.

144 According to a representative of ACICS, upon inquiry by the author.

145 Nasson Institute, "Nasson Institute newsletter," (1991). Affirmed by a representative of ACCET in 2012, upon inquiry by the author.

146 John Gold, "Nasson College Graduation Is New Beginning," *Journal Tribune*, July 28, 1986.

degree he earned. He said it was not a watered-down MBA program, and his degree had not just been given away.[147]

Jim Elliott attended Nasson College from 1986 to 1987. He originally attended Fitchburg State College in Massachusetts and then went to work in Kennebunk, Maine. He enrolled in Nasson's MBA program and graduated in 1987. He found the work to be challenging, and noted that the program relied on the same textbooks used at other schools. He had nine or ten different professors during his two years at Nasson and found all of them to be well qualified. He said they would fail a student if the student did not produce quality work. He went on to attend Husson University in Maine, which accepted his credits from Nasson College. There, he earned his BS in accounting; eventually he received a master of arts in economic development from the University of Massachusetts.[148]

As for the admissions process, Elliott said he provided a high school transcript, but he was also asked about his work experience, as this was a graduate-level program. He found the students to be of a high caliber, noting that all had had significant work experience before attending.

Elliott said everyone at the school believed the institution was accredited by someone, though not NEASC. There was some discussion about another accrediting body, but he did not know which. He did know that the state of Maine still allowed degree-granting authority to the college. He was not aware of any undergraduate students. He had some classes in Brown Hall, which he recalls as clean and well kept. Students, he said, had no complaints. The gym and other buildings were not in use.

Elliot defended Mattar, saying he believed that Mattar was doing what he could to increase revenue while the college rebuilt itself. While some students were boarding in Marland Hall, Mattar also wanted to rent rooms to nonstudents, but the town would not let him. As time went on, Elliott said, Mattar and the town lost trust in each other.

The New Nasson College Begins to Fall Apart

By the late 1980s, about one hundred students were connected to Nasson.[149] Lou D'Allesandro, who was president of Nasson College from 1986 to 1987, said that they really were trying to build a school there, and that they were succeeding. For example, the students were eligible for federally

---

147 Gold, "Nasson College Graduation."
148 Jim Elliott, in interview with the author, January 19, 2012.
149 Hoar, "Nasson Begins Process."

guaranteed student loans and the federal Pell Grant Program.[150] And yet Mattar would instruct him to do something like sell the portrait hanging on the wall of Marland Hall without offering any explanation. Barbara Holt, the administrative coordinator at Nasson, said that Mattar treated people terribly. If you crossed him, he would either totally ignore you or pound his fist on the table, telling you how stupid you were. Meetings would go on and on, and still you never could figure out exactly what he was trying to do or what he wanted.[151]

At one point, the school did produce a more complete catalog that was almost worthy of the label. It gave Nasson's history and its new mission. It included lists of courses and discussed ways students could earn academic credits. Tuition and fees were forty dollars per credit hour and a thirty-five-dollar application fee. The school's application asked for students' education records[152] and provided a transcript request form the applicant could send to previous schools. According to this catalog, "Nasson College is a non-profit institution chartered by the State of Maine to grant associate, bachelor, master and doctoral degrees."

THE ALUMNI ASSOCIATION STRUGGLES TO SURVIVE

"Nasson Lives!" This was the headline in the *Nasson Alumni News* August 1989.[153] The one-page newsletter was the first mass mailing to alumni since the school had closed. It quickly and succinctly tried to bring everyone up to date on events of the intervening years. It provided a bit of a chronology of events since the school had closed, and contained this happy announcement:

> December, 1984 – A miracle! One Edward P. Mattar III arrives in the nick of time and purchases the core campus intact! His plan ... to reopen Nasson College!

---

150 Ibid.

151 Mark Shanahan, "Nasson's 'Savior' Writes New Chapter," *Maine Sunday Telegram*, December 14, 1997.

152 The catalog's note on the subject of education records advised prospective students, "Please list all schools you have attended starting with high school and ending with the most recent school you have attended. Please indicate the dates attended, the number of college semester credit hours earned, and the type of credential you received from each school (diploma, GED, certificate, associate degree). A student will not be accepted until official transcripts are received from each school."

153 Nasson College Alumni Association, *Nasson Alumni News*, August 1989.

Upper Campus, Pryor-Hussey, Folsom, Hilltop House, and Deering Pond are sold.

July, 1985 – more than two years after the closing, Nasson reopens to welcome the next generation of students.

The newsletter admitted, "While it may be premature to say that Nasson is thriving, we are pleased to note that, more than four years after its rebirth, Nasson is certainly holding its own! Come see!"[154] Other items of note related to the redevelopment of Main Street in Springvale (often referred to as the *destruction* of Main Street by some opponents of the redevelopment). The newsletter mentioned that all the shops on Main Street, once home to Vic Remy's Market, Down Maine House, and Normans, were all gone and the lots had been vacant for more than a decade, though plans to build a shopping strip there were announced. Allen Hall was reported to have been recently renovated (but there was no evidence to support that), and the Science Center was the temporary home of Springvale Elementary School.

Elaine Bean succeeded Robert Stone as president of the alumni association. She recognized that, with the demise of the college, the association needed reorganization. New bylaws were written, and the association changed from a council of officers to a board of directors. Henceforth, alumni association membership would be open to all graduates of Nasson Institute or Nasson College, all students who attended the New Division at Nasson, anyone who attended Nasson for one semester or more, honorary degree recipients, former trustees, former faculty and administrative staff, and all former office and secretarial staff, kitchen/dining staff, and buildings and grounds staff. By definition and intentionally, this included students who attended Mattar's school. That year, 143 alumni, faculty, and staff members attended homecoming.[155]

USE OF OTHER BUILDINGS

In June 1988, the town approved plans to convert Alumni Hall into twelve one-bedroom apartments, at a cost of $325,000. According to David Joy, architect for the conversion, the exterior would be upgraded and new windows installed, but the existing facade would not be changed.[156]

154 Ibid.
155 Nasson College Alumni Association, *Nasson Alumni News*, February 1989.
156 C. Scott Hoar, "Nasson Building Conversion OK'd," *Portland Press Herald*, June

Allen Hall almost found a new life too. Mark Kearns, owner of the Shawmut Inn, sought to use the hall for employee housing. Kearns's idea was to bring in forty-seven employees from Alabama for the summer. Working with Jobs Unlimited of Wells, the inn hoped to bring in up to 117 employees, all of whom needed housing.[157] Kearns said that, not only would this be good for the employees, it would be an economic benefit for the town. He began renovating the dorm in anticipation of its use. Rosemary Guptil, director of Jobs Unlimited, agreed that the housing proposal was critical to her program.

However, code officials from the town said that they would need a conditional use permit before workers could be housed there. Under the town's view, the proposed use would be that of a boarding or rooming house, and that required prior approval and a hearing from the planning board. It was all too much. The idea faded away.

Unused campus buildings began attracting attention from townspeople. As early as 1988, people began to see that Mattar was not acting in a manner consistent with the campus's intended educational use. In the opinion of at least one person, Joel Plourde, Mattar had "reneged on his moral and legal commitment made to the residents of the Sanford-Springvale communities three years ago when he pledged to 'revitalize the College.'" Plourde said that turning the college into a boarding house was hardly meeting that commitment. He claimed that, since Mattar had come to town, he "has done little except to continually challenge, resist, and defy the Town of Sanford, which helped him to finance the venture in the first place."[158] The writer urged the town to enforce the zoning laws, not ignore or amend them.

"August 1989: Nasson College 75th Commencement" read the program for the event. With a modified Nasson College seal on the cover, the program implied there was a genuine graduation from a genuine college. There were a processional, an invocation, welcomes, presentation of awards, a commencement address, and the conferring of degrees and certificates by Board of Trustees Chairman Edward Paul Mattar III. The event concluded with a benediction and a recessional, to the tune of "Pomp and Circumstance." Degrees handed out were for masters of business administration (nineteen students), bachelors of science (one student), and associates of science (three students). Certificates were also awarded for

---

15, 1988.

157 C. Scott Hoar, "Officials Debate Use of Nasson's Allen Hall," *Portland Press Herald*, June 16, 1988. It's not clear who those employees would have been working for.

158 Joel Plourde, Letter to the Editor, "Use of Nasson College," *Portland Press Herald*, July 20, 1988.

Computer-Based Accounting, Office Information Systems, Supervision and Management, Work Processing Specialist, and Office Automation Specialist. Twenty-five students received certificates. In all, forty-eight graduated.

At the alumni homecoming in October 1989, one of the alumni went into the library where the new college was housed. No one there knew anything about the old Nasson College. They had no brochures or catalogs of the new school, but one worker said they hoped to have catalogs printed sometime in the future. They said the school had about sixty students. At that point, there were no communications between alumni of the old school and the new school.

NASSON COLLEGE LOOKS FOR ITS OWN IDENTITY

Another development arose. In addition to "Nasson College," there was now also "Nasson Institute," which was reported to have 150 students. The school, such as it was, had moved out of the Anderson Learning Center and into the Science Center. Nasson Institute was a proprietary school operated by Mattar. It would seem that Nasson Institute, described as a proprietary school (in other words, for profit), was a different corporate entity from Nasson College.

In 1985, Nasson Institute teamed up with Cornerstone Owner Builder Schools, an existing program that offered programs for people who wanted to be involved in the construction of their own homes. Though Cornerstone relocated to the Nasson campus, the two programs seemed to keep their separate identities, and Cornerstone was never mentioned in Nasson's catalogs.

The graduation program for August 1990 now showed "Nasson Institute and Nasson College" on the cover, with no distinction or explanation inside. Then in 1991, the school produced a publication that promoted both Nasson College and Nasson Institute. According to the newsletter, the college would open for the fall on September 30, 1991, for both degree- and nondegree-seeking students. Twenty-seven different courses were offered. New subjects were one-act play production, news writing, weaving for beginners, women's history, creative writing, critical contemporary family issues, and integrated arts. As before, a full schedule of business courses was offered. One feature article addressed the fact that military service or job training could actually qualify students for college credits. Identifying all the college credits students had earned outside the school would enable them to complete their college degree in a shorter time. Nasson still required 120 semester hours to receive a bachelor of arts degree (though BA recipients did not appear in the graduation programs). Nasson would help students determine all the credits they may have earned through work and then tailor the remainder of their program to the students' interests and needs. Students could take classes by correspondence, directed or independent study, by television, or on-site in traditional classroom settings. All courses were three credit hours, and cost $120 per course. No mention was made of accreditation. And though one registered for degree or no degree, there was no mention of exactly what degree a graduate would qualify for.

Sometimes the school seemed to be flailing around. A big advertisement, not dated, listed three locations in Maine—Springvale, Portland, and Caribou! "Learning was never like this ... until now! ... At Nasson College we give you more than a catalog, fancy brochures and applications to complete. Our trained admissions representatives will help you look at where you've been, where you are now and how to prepare for your future ... We've been preparing students like you for business careers since 1912. Now, we are preparing our students in business careers for today and into the year 2000."

It was advertised for "Adults Only!"

On the other side of the publication—it was two-sided, with two front pages that flipped—was a promotion for Nasson Institute, though there was no explanation to distinguish the two. Institute students also graduated, but there was no mention of degrees. On the other hand, Nasson Institute was accredited by the Accrediting Council for Continuing Education & Training (ACCET). Financial aid was available; Pell grants, Stafford loans, and PLUS loans were all potentially available to students. Classes and costs were not shown.

Bit by bit, things began to decline on campus. In Marland Hall, Mattar began operating a sort of rooming house for low-income Sanford-Springvale residents, renting rooms to people and giving them vouchers to attend his school, thus allowing them to masquerade as students. The town saw through this and objected, arguing that he was using the dormitory for noneducational purposes. Mattar began to sell off the library's books, periodicals, and reference materials. Although his lease with the town permitted him to sell any of the books not needed to support the curriculum, the money was supposed to be reinvested in the educational program. By the early 1990s, the library had been gutted of almost everything of value.[159]

---

159 Shanahan, "Nasson's 'Savior.'"

On November 30, 1992, Fred Douglas, director of higher education services for the Maine Department of Education, conducted an on-site inspection of Nasson. By that time, Nasson was not accepting students, and it had not been for some time; nor was it promoting the institution or even recruiting students. Only two students were then enrolled at Nasson, both as correspondence students. There was no staff or faculty, and none of the buildings on campus were in use in any way by Nasson College.

Following Douglas's visit, the state of Maine sent several letters to Mattar inquiring about the current activities of Nasson. The letters were not answered. Finally, an action was commenced by the Maine State Board of Education to determine whether or not the authority of Nasson to confer degrees should be terminated because Nasson had substantially discontinued instruction. Mattar, who was still chairman of the board of trustees, signed a consent order dated April 13, 1993. Thus, Nasson voluntarily relinquished its degree-granting authority, effective May 31, 1993—just over ten years after Nasson had originally ceased operations.[160]

As a result of the consent order, Nasson was no longer entitled to use the word *college* in its name. So it may be said that the day that Nasson College finally ceased to exist was not May 2, 1983, but May 31, 1993.[161]

Still, if it wanted to, Nasson could apply to the state Board of Education for a certificate of temporary approval to use the terms *junior college*, *college*, or *university* in its name or to reapply for degree-granting authority. As of January 10, 1994, Nasson had never done so.[162]

Mattar's Nasson Institute was not affected by the withdrawal of the college's degree-granting authority. With its limited accreditation, it could confer "certificates of proficiency" but not two- or four-year degrees.[163] The institute, which had never had any degree-granting authority, was at one time located in the Science Center. In 1996, the institute left the Nasson campus, renamed itself the Career Institute, and moved to the

---

160 Brent Macey, "Panel to Take Degree Grant from College," *Portland Press Herald*, April 14, 1993.

161 According to a representative of the Maine Department of Secretary of State, Bureau of Corporations, Nasson's license was last suspended on July 15, 1996. The official said that, while Nasson's charter had been suspended on numerous occasions over the years, it had been reinstated each time.

162 *Hanscom* 93E-0080 at 22.

163 Jeff Ward, "Nasson May Lose Degree Powers," *Portland Press Herald*, March 9, 1993.

South Sanford Center for Shopping.[164] Eventually, its incorporation was suspended, effective July 22, 1992.[165]

It was the Finance Authority of Maine (FAME) that finally forced the shutdown of the Career Institute. Mattar had refused to pay $75,000 in refunds to students who withdrew from the program early.[166] At that point, more than one hundred students were left with incomplete training, outstanding loans, and dim prospects for transfer or employment, according to FAME.

While all that was going on, Key Bank foreclosed on Alumni Hall. Alumni Hall was one of the buildings Mattar had purchased in 1984. He had borrowed $450,000 from Key Bank.[167] Also, the town had $22,734 in tax liens pending against five buildings owned or controlled by Mattar.[168]

But with Mattar finally off campus—off campus, but not gone—none of the main campus buildings were being used, heated, or maintained, and they all began to deteriorate.

In the fall of 1993, the town considered spending money to preserve them. The problem was that, although the town owned the Anderson Learning Center, Mattar still controlled the rest of the buildings. After the college moved out, the buildings were no longer maintained at all. The roofs began to leak, and the interiors suffered damage from lack of heat during the winter.[169] But since Mattar still held a lease on the library, townspeople were concerned and indignant that Mattar might benefit from the improvements.[170]

---

164 Royal Ford, "Benefactor's Intent at Issue on Trust Tug of War," *Boston Sunday Globe*, October 3, 1993; Brent Macey, "Three Plans Outline Nasson Campus Reuse," *Portland Press Herald*, September 8, 1993.

165 *Hanscom* 93E-0080 at 20.

166 "FAME Joins Outcry Over Sale of Buildings," *Portland Press Herald*, December 10, 1997.

167 Ted Cohen, "Bank Sues Trustees for Nasson Default," *Portland Press Herald*, July 22, 1993.

168 The foreclosure auction in March 1994 brought in a top bid of only $150,000, less than the minimum bid sought by the bank of $190,000. Brent Macey, "Sanford Uses Default Claim in Fight over Nasson Lease," *Portland Press Herald*, March 16, 1994.

169 Brent Macey, "Sanford Seeking to Fix Up College," *Portland Press Herald*, October 6, 1993.

170 Brent Macey, "Town Delays Plan to Fix Nasson Roof," *Portland Press Herald*, November 18, 1993.

3

A POT OF GOLD

HOMECOMING ACTIVITIES BEGAN TO be larger and better organized in the early 1990s. The 1993 reunion was held on October 2. Alumni set up a big tent on the campus quad, and provided popcorn, beer, wine, and other beverages. Of great importance, but without providing any details, was this note sent to alumni: "The current administration is gone and many parties have an interest in purchasing [the college]. The alumni association needs your input while it establishes a relationship with the new owners."[171] Captain Prosser's history of Nasson College was finally published and available for sale.

The reference to "many parties" became evident at the afternoon gathering. Two or three visitors to the event made presentations, expressing their individual plans to reestablish Nasson College, again. One of them was an aviation school called Air-Tech Inc., located in Limerick, Maine. Another presentation was made by Nasson's eternal friend and supporter, Dean Mac, James J. McLaughlin. He proposed creating a new school on the old campus, to be named Springvale College. Upon a question from someone in the audience, Dean Mac acknowledged that he would be interested in retaining the name Nasson College, if that were possible.[172]

What became very evident in both presentations was something that most people had been unaware of. A substantial trust fund, payable to

---

171 Nasson College Alumni Association, postcard, "Homecoming '93," 1993.
172 See Brent Macey, "Nine Parties Vie for Trust Fund Left to Nasson," *Portland Press Herald*, September 21, 1993. Of course at that point, it was not possible. Mattar still controlled the name "Nasson College."

Nasson College, was about to come due. Without the old Nasson College around, where it would go was a hot topic of discussion.[173]

Some more backstory is required.

A man named Hervey A. Hanscom was born on December 18, 1867, in Lebanon, Maine. In 1890, he graduated from the Gorham Normal School, which later became the University of Southern Maine (USM).[174] Hanscom moved to Medford, Massachusetts, in 1895, where he lived until his death in 1968. In 1954, Hanscom established two scholarship funds, one at Tuft's College and one at the Gorham Normal School, both scholarships bearing his name. Income from the original gift of $6,000 to Tufts was intended to provide financial assistance to "a deserving boy, preferably a country boy from Maine."[175] The Gorham/USM scholarship was originally endowed with a gift of 20 shares of AT&T stock (which, after splits, had grown to 274 shares). The income from the USM scholarship was to provide financial assistance to students from Sanford, Springvale, and Lebanon, Maine, who attended the university. Hanscom also made other charitable gifts.

Hanscom never married and had no children, though he did have nieces and nephews and other relatives, some of whom he provided for in his will. Hanscom's will was dated September 27, 1962, and had been revised several times. The last revision was dated August 26, 1965. Through his will, Hanscom showed his interest in assisting young people to finance their education.

Nasson College was named as an alternative charitable beneficiary of a $100,000 gift under Article III of the will. But this bequest was deleted by Hanscom's first codicil in 1965. Nevertheless, Nasson College was named, and remained, the residuary beneficiary of Hanscom's estate. The gift was to go directly to Nasson College upon his death, to establish the Hervey A. Hanscom Scholarship Fund. The fund was to be used for the purpose of providing scholarships for worthy undergraduate students, preferably those students who resided in the towns of Sanford and Lebanon, Maine. Specifically, the will directed his trustees:

> To hold, manage, invest, and reinvest the principal and
> all accumulations of income thereof as a fund for the
> benefit of Nasson College, an educational institution
> organized by law and located at Springvale, in the Town

---

173 Nasson College officials had always been aware of the existence of the trust and recognized that it could be a huge problem solver in its later years. While the school made efforts to accelerate the payout of the trust, it was not successful.

174 *Hanscom* 93E-0080.

175 *Hanscom* 93E-0080, at 4.

of Sanford, County of York, State of Maine, for a period
of twenty-five (25) years from the date of my decease.
Upon expiration of such period of time, the Trustees shall
pay over, deliver, assign, transfer or convey to said Nasson
College the entire principal and accumulated income of
this trust fund. Thereafter, Nasson College shall hold this
fund as a part of its capital endowment and shall use the
net income thereof only for the general purposes of the
College. This fund shall be established and known as the
"Hervey A. Hanscom Fund."[176]

There was no "gift-over" in the event that the residuary bequest to
Nasson College failed. At the time the will was admitted to the probate
court after Hanscom died, the estate was worth $348,648.43.

There is no record that Hervey Hanscom or any of his relatives ever
attended Nasson College. No record shows that Hanscom ever even *visited*
Nasson College.

The trust, by its own terms, was to terminate on June 3, 1993, and its
proceeds turned over to Nasson College. At the time it became due, the
value of the trust was more than $2 million, with an annual income of
about $60,000.[177]

At the time Hanscom wrote his will, Nasson was a viable small liberal
arts college. By the time the trust matured, Nasson was gone.

The probate court noted that the well-settled law of Massachusetts[178]
is that, when the named beneficiary is not capable of carrying out the
donor's charitable intention, the specific charitable purpose of the trust
will be deemed impossible of fulfillment and the named beneficiary will
not be entitled to the gift of the trust property. Therefore, the court ruled
that the public charitable purpose served by the provision in the trust under
the will of Hervey A. Hanscom for the benefit of Nasson College became
"impossible of fulfillment" and that Nasson College was not entitled to the
gift of the trust property.[179]

Consequently, lots of people and institutions applied to be the new
beneficiary. Applicants included the Lenox School, the University of New
England, the town of Sanford, John Barth, Maine Community Foundation
Inc., the University of Maine System, Southern Maine Technical College,
Air-Tech Inc., Husson College, the attorney general of Massachusetts,

---

176 Ibid, 8; language directly from Hanscom's will.
177 Ibid, 8–10.
178 Hanscom died in Massachusetts, and the will was executed there.
179 *Hanscom* 93E-0080, "Decision."

Nasson College Alumni Association, and Nasson College itself (which was still a corporate entity controlled by Mattar).[180]

Mattar's timing was a little off.[181] In April 1993, Nasson's charter and its degree-granting authority had been withdrawn by the state Board of Education. Had Nasson still been in business two months later, it is quite possible the trust would have gone to the school.[182]

Eventually, the trust went to the University of Maine System, under the condition that it establish a scholarship fund for York County students, with preference shown to applicants from Sanford and Lebanon.[183] Some of the money was given to renovate the Anderson Learning Center.[184] In awarding the trust to UMS, the court denied appeals for the money from the University of New England in Biddeford, Husson College in Bangor, and Tufts College in Medford, Massachusetts.

With the collapse of any chance to receive the trust funds, all of the other plans for new schools faded away.[185]

The town still could not do anything with the learning center, because Mattar still held a lease on the building, at one dollar per year. However, one of the terms of the lease was that *actual educational activities* be taking place at the building. After more than twelve months had passed without such activity, the town served notice to Mattar that he was in default.[186]

Mattar let his opinion of that action be very clear. He cut down a long row of bushes that grew along Main Street in Springvale.[187] He served notice on the town that he intended to demolish the gym, the Little

---

180 Macey, "Nine Parties Vie."

181 It is fair to wonder whether Mattar had been aware of the trust fund all along and had only become involved with Nasson College in the hope that, eventually, he would be able to get his hands on it. Alas, nothing in the record sheds any light on this theory.

182 Macey, "Nine Parties Vie."

183 During the first five years of Hanscom scholarships, the University of Maine System awarded $772,750 to 374 students from York County, Maine. Of those, 182 students were from Sanford and Lebanon and received $465,750.

184 Mark Shanahan, "Nasson Trust Goes to UMaine System," *Portland Press Herald*, July 14, 1995, 1.

185 The proposed Springvale College continued its efforts to become an established school. In March 1994, representatives of the new college engaged in discussions with Kittery officials to lease the Wentworth-Dennett school building. Brent Macey, "Kittery Offers College a Home," *Portland Press Herald*, March 9, 1994; Chris Cleaveland, "Springvale College Eyes Kittery School," *Star*, March 1994.

186 Brent Macey, "Sanford Uses Default Claim in Fight over Nasson Lease," *Portland Press Herald*, March 16, 1994.

187 Brent Macey, "College Caretaker Cuts down Shrubbery," *Portland Press Herald*, March 16, 1994.

Theatre, the dining commons, Allen Hall, and Brown Hall. Since Mattar had not provided all the specifications on demolition—such as a disposal plan—the town denied the permits.

But Mattar kept at it. In April 1994, he rototilled campus lawns. He cut down maple trees that bordered the Springvale Library. He dumped cow manure on the lawn in front of Brown Hall. He painted Folsom Hall red, white, and blue. He never mowed the lawns, and he forbade the town from doing so. He emptied some of "his"[188] buildings of their contents—clearing out desks, chairs, books, lamps, tables, dishes, and more. The stuff was put in a parking lot on Main Street, and he let anyone haul anything away. All his actions were legal; he still controlled the buildings and their contents.[189]

Marland Hall was being used for low-income housing, but in August 1994, the tenants were told to leave because, according to Mattar's representative, there were not enough of them to pay for the upkeep of the building.[190] And about this time, Mattar was selling, giving away, or just trashing most of the books remaining in the library, which actually belonged to the town. Left were the books no one wanted, the books without any special value. Plastic tarps covered the shelves, protecting books from the leaking roof.[191] Finally, in August 1995, the town just auctioned off what was left of the books. Most of them were purchased by two book dealers, Frank Wood of De Wolfe & Wood in Alfred, Maine, and Merv Slotnick of East Coast Books. John Barth, who was planning a new school on the upper campus, also bought some of the collection, as did the town of Lyman, which was planning to build a new library.

But it wasn't Mattar that almost took out one of the old Nasson buildings. On the morning of April 15, 1994, fire broke out in the old Seminar Building on Main Street in Springvale. The fire evidently started while the building was being renovated into apartments. The building, one of the oldest buildings in Springvale, suffered significant damage but remained structurally sound. It was fully repaired.

---

188 The concept of ownership was always messy. Mattar did not own Nasson College; he just controlled it. That distinction was to come to a head in 1997.

189 Brent Macey, "Nasson College Items Given Away," *Portland Press Herald*, April 29, 1994.

190 Ann Fisher, "They're Out of Marland Hall Effective August 24," *Sanford News*, August 23, 1994.

191 Mark Shanahan, "Deserted Library's Books Languish," *Portland Press Herald*, April 10, 1995.

PAST DEEDS BEGIN TO CLOSE IN ON MATTAR

The 1994 Alumni homecoming was set for October 22. At that time, the campus was not available for homecoming activities. The annual meeting was held at 3:00 p.m. at the Sanford Country Club (now the Sanford Golf Club). Following the meeting was a buffet dinner. "Come early for the music and merriments and stay on for the buffet." Music was provided by Stoney of America Music Services. Copies of Prosser's book were available for purchase.

By October 1994, Nasson had failed to make any payments to the US Department of Education for Allen Hall, Marland Hall, or the Science Center. Consequently, the department initiated foreclosure proceedings on those buildings. Town officials were ecstatic at the possibility that Mattar might finally be forced out and said the action could open future possibilities for the campus.[192]

More backstory seems prudent. After Mattar took over Nasson College in 1985, Nasson executed and delivered to Key Bank (successor to Canal Bank), what were essentially two second mortgages on Allen Hall and Marland Hall.[193] But by 1994, they were in default. The bank accelerated the debt and demanded that the debt be cured. When it was not, Key Trust (which had taken over Key Bank) then filed a complaint for foreclosure by civil action on January 20, 1995, alleging that Nasson had defaulted on its obligations. Key Trust was unable to serve Nasson and two parties-in-interest, so on March 14, 1995, it received an ex parte order allowing service by publication. The trial court granted Key Trust's motion for summary judgment and a default judgment on August 15, 1995.[194]

It was not until almost a year later that Nasson responded. On March 14, 1996, Nasson filed a motion for relief from judgment pursuant to state law. It seems Key Trust had failed to serve the secretary of state, resulting in the court's voiding the previously entered judgment of foreclosure. On

---

192 Brent Macey, "Nasson Buildings Face Foreclosure," *Portland Press Herald*, September 7, 1994.

193 *Key Trust Co. of Maine v. Nasson College*, 697 A.2d at 408 (1997). Specifically, "On March 20, 1985, Nasson executed and delivered to Key Bank of Southern Maine, as successor trustee to Canal National Bank, two first supplemental indenture and bondholder consents amending the prior indenture of mortgage and deed of trust documents. Key Trust notified Nasson on November 23, 1994, that the supplemental indentures were in default, accelerated the debt, and demanded that the debt be cured. Key Trust filed a complaint for foreclosure by civil action on January 20, 1995, alleging that Nasson had defaulted on its obligations as provided by the supplemental indentures." 694 A.2d at 409.

194 *Id.*

May 10, 1996, the court entered an order setting forth a pretrial schedule. The court ordered that discovery be completed by June 30, 1996.[195]

Nasson filed an answer to the suit on May 30, 1996. While Nasson admitted that it had failed to make payments, it claimed that that failure did not constitute a default. Further, Nasson claimed that Key Trust had failed to state a claim on which relief could be granted and had waived its right to collect sums pursuant to the supplemental indentures.

On August 1, 1996, Key Trust again filed a motion for summary judgment and a default judgment and to dismiss parties-in-interest, along with a statement of material facts and an accompanying affidavit. Nasson opposed the motion and filed its own statement of material facts and an accompanying affidavit signed by Mattar. After a hearing, the court granted Key Trust's motions and entered a finding for Key Trust.[196] Again.

On appeal, Nasson argued that it was relying on the defense of estoppel or forbearance, claiming that Key Trust was precluded from enforcing the provisions of the loan documents because of certain alleged promises and representations made to Nasson at the time the supplemental indentures were executed. Although not explicitly stated, Mattar argued that Nasson had relied on those promises. Nasson raised an issue of material fact as to the existence of a promise that may have been made with regard to the federal government's intention not to foreclose in the event of a default, but it failed to demonstrate any evidence of its reliance on the alleged promise. That failure blocked Nasson's claim as a matter of law.[197] The decision of the court was upheld. Key Trust had the right to foreclose on Nasson.

WHAT TO DO WITH THE CAMPUS?

Back in the early 1990s, the town had commissioned several studies to try to figure out what to do with the campus, if and when Mattar ever left.

One of the first reports was issued by Winton Scott Architects in August 1993.[198] The firm's study focused on the Anderson Learning Center, which the town owned. Winton Scott acknowledged that the building was then in fairly good condition. The main problem, Winton thought, was that, if the building were converted from use as a library to an office building, many changes would be necessary because of increased occupancy. Among the

---

195 *Id.*

196 *Id.*

197 *Id.* at 12-13.

198 Mark Wilcox, Principal of Winton Scott Architects, letter to Richard Wilkins, Sanford Public Works Director, August 18, 1993.

issues that would have to be dealt with were the removal of underground oil storage tanks, increased electric service, improvements to Bodwell Court, and storm drains. The roof needed replacing, the windows were not energy efficient, the basement needed new ventilators, and the building would have to be air-conditioned.[199] There were handicap access issues. The ramp in front was not in compliance with standards, doors needed to have all new locking hardware, and an elevator would have to be installed. The floor tiles probably contained asbestos. Parking would have to be substantially increased. For an office building that size, code would require 100 to 136 parking spaces, which would have a significant impact on the existing grass quadrangle, including the loss of many mature trees. The total estimated cost to make all these improvements was $530,000.

In March 1994, Market Decisions, a research and planning firm, issued its own study, "A Preliminary Market Assessment for the Possible Reuse of Space on the Former Nasson College Campus." According to this report, the goal was to determine the potential interest of public or private educational uses in the library or other buildings on the campus. The firm looked at possible use by public schools, colleges, or universities; specialized educational or training schools for disabled individuals; preschools; adult and continuing education institutions; or other private or parochial schools. Overall, Market Decisions concluded there was no likely interest from public or private schools. The firm did find some interest from postsecondary schools. Most promising was a possible University of Maine/Sanford Center branch or a vocational college, such as York County Technical College or the Southern Maine Technical College. As for private colleges, the consultants spoke with Hesser College, Mid State College, Andover College, and the University of New England. Some expressed interest, but none was interested in establishing a major operation in Springvale. Some specialty schools, such as beauty schools or aviation-related schools, which could be tied in to Sanford Airport operations, also expressed interest. The report suggested that demand for the use of 15,000 to 25,000 square feet of space in the next year may exist, with demand for an additional 10,000 to 15,000 square feet arising in two or three years.

---

199 In fact, the library had been a mess from the day it was built. The building, built in 1961 (with an addition in 1970), was designed with little thought for energy conservation, and was built at low cost, without consideration of the related long-term costs. It was steel-frame construction, but the columns were not fire protected. No sprinkler system existed, and much of the building had an extensive amount of single-glazed, steel-curtain wall construction, which made the building costly to heat. Memorandum from Dick Eustis, UMaine System, to Sheri Stevens, October 13, 1992.

The study identified many potential office uses. It suggested that state agencies located in Alfred and Sanford might be consolidated on the campus and noted that the Southern Maine Regional Planning Commission needed to add to the 1,200 square feet it currently had in Sanford. Other potential users had issues with Nasson's location, accessibility, and cost. The consultants noted that rental of the facility by numerous small users instead of one large one would result in an increased need for more day-to-day management of the facility, which would increase costs.

Next, the consultants looked at other buildings on the campus, principally the Little Theatre and the gymnasium. They noted that the area lacked sufficient recreational and cultural facilities and a general lack of space for performances, large meetings, dinners, or similar functions. The need was generally met by use of school facilities. But while use of school buildings would keep costs down, there were inherent problems, as outside users would have to work around school activities and weekend and summertime access would be limited. The consultants recognized that, in order to make the best use of the gym or theater, there should be a prime tenant, but interest among local arts organizations was limited.

Market Design thought that the best chance for a large successful operation on campus would be to loosely emulate the Portland Expo Center, which was owned by the city of Portland. In its early years, the center was mostly used for sporting events, and it lost money. The city repurposed the facility, hired staff, and turned it into a multiuse facility. While it was still used for sporting events, it was also available for trade shows, banquets, dances, and concerts. (Notably, the consultants did not say that the Expo Center had been transformed into a moneymaking operation.)

In 1993, the town had created the Nasson College Community Development Advisory Committee, which was chaired by Gary Sullivan and Anna Ashley. The committee issued its report, entitled "Rebirth of a Campus: A Maine Community Development Block Grant Proposal" in June 1994. At that time, the town owned the library, but Nasson College (in other words, Mattar) still owned Allen Hall, Marland Hall, Brown Hall, the gym, the Little Theatre, the dining commons, and the Science Center. In short, the "Rebirth" analysis addressed many of the same issues raised by both of the previous studies, but was perhaps more thorough. The study recommended that the area be redeveloped in two phases—first, the library and then, other buildings.[200]

---

200 Nasson College Community Development Advisory Committee (NCCDAC), "Rebirth of a Campus: A Maine Community Development Block Grant Proposal," June 1994, 5.

As for the library, the study also recognized a need to have an anchor tenant, such as the University of Maine System or the York County Technical College (which was part of the Southern Maine Technical College). The committee recommended that some of the space on the ground level be dedicated to community use. The study reviewed many of the same issues addressed by the previous reports, such as parking, removal of the underground oil tank, electricity, accessibility (including installation of an elevator), and more. The total cost to redevelop the library this time was estimated at $445,000.[201]

Phase II would be the rebirth of the rest of the old college campus. The goal was to make it a center of educational and cultural activities for the Sanford-Springvale community. The committee looked at each of the main buildings and evaluated each one's potential for productive use.

Brown Hall, the first dormitory for the original Nasson Institute in the early 1900s, later used for classrooms and administration, was best suited for office use, but it lacked adequate parking.

The Memorial Student Activity Center included the gym, theater, and dining commons. The gym was to be used by many community groups and not to be the exclusive home to anyone. The dining commons could be a conference center and location of large-scale functions, which had no existing space in town. The Little Theatre was in poor condition, and the committee recommended that it be torn down.

Allen Hall, originally a men's dormitory, was in poor physical condition. Its only future use would be as the site of a parking lot—the building would have to be torn down.

Marland Hall was originally a girls' dormitory, but it also had dining facilities within it. It could be used for a school's hospitality and tourism programs or as housing for a conference center. Noneducational uses could include low-income housing or an elder hostel.

The Science Center could be used by the York County Technical College as a facility for research and development or as a grade school.

As for how all this might come to pass, the Rebirth committee suggested that the town obtain ownership of all of the campus buildings and then establish a nonprofit organization to manage them.[202]

The committee recognized that public support would be essential in carrying out any of these proposals. Therefore, the committee sought public opinion in a variety of ways, including a public forum, an opinion poll, and a town-meeting survey. In principle, most people were in favor of the

---

201 NCCDAC, "Rebirth," 9.
202 NCCDAC, "Rebirth," 13.

proposals, but few were eager to see tax dollars fund it. Instead, the idea of a municipal bond to be repaid by revenues from tenants found more favor.

Several times during this period, the Maine Technical College System considered locating at Nasson. Each time, however, the MTCS decided against it. Nasson was said to be too small and too far from the Maine Turnpike. Instead, the school selected a location in Wells. But that was not easy going either. There were issues with wetlands at the proposed site, and funding for a new building was delayed or insufficient. The school had lower than expected enrollment, but it was depending on tuition and fees to pay for construction. The state was expected to pay about $1.2 million a year in operating costs. The school repeatedly rejected the Nasson site, arguing that it would cost more to rehabilitate the buildings than it would to build all new buildings in Wells.[203]

The University of Maine in Augusta expressed interest. At the time, the university was renting space at Sanford Center, but that lease was set to expire in September 1994. The university was interested in the Nasson campus, provided the buildings were redeveloped by the town, at the town's expense.[204]

Goodall Hospital in Sanford considered using Marland Hall for residential care. Air-Tech Inc., the aviation maintenance school, was also interested in using Marland Hall as a student residence. Among the reasons for their interest in that location was "the proximity of the campus to downtown community institutions—church, library, coffee shop, drugstore, post office, banks, hairdresser, book store, restaurants, etc."[205]

There was some movement in other properties. In July 1996, local Sanford contractor Robert Reinken was reported to be considering buying Brown Hall. The land around Deering Pond, once known as the Russell Environmental Studies Tract, had been sold to Robert Hall in 1982. His wife gave it to the Sanford-Springvale Mousam Way Land Trust in 1995.[206]

The college library was finally renovated in 1995. After the books and shelving were disposed of and with Mattar now out of the way, the space was at last available for development. The town ended up spending $1 million for repairs and improvements.[207]

---

203 Mark Shanahan, "Technical College Urged to Move," *Portland Press Herald*, February 10, 1996; Mark Shanahan, "Board Rules out Nasson for College," *Portland Press Herald*, March 22, 1996.

204 Letter from George Connick, president of the University of Maine, to Allan Mapes, July 26, 1993.

205 Town of Sanford, "The Rebirth of the Nasson College Campus," Interim Report, April 4, 1995.

206 *Nasson News* (Winter 2005).

207 Mark Shanahan, "Man with a Plan," *Portland Press Herald*, August 17, 1995.

The University of Maine System was the first to move into the Anderson Learning Center (the library). The ALC included a state-of-the-art computer lab and a small new browsing library in a comfortable educational setting. The center's one-page catalog listed fifty-three classes. Among them were Human Sexuality, Religions of the World, Foundations of Criminal Justice, Social Psychology, Statistics, and many more.[208] As with U Maine's predecessor, Nasson College (Mattar's Nasson), students could attend days or evenings and take credit or noncredit courses. Also, as with Nasson, there were interactive television courses. Admissions? Not a lot of detail. "Make an Appointment *now* with an academic advisor to discuss your professional and academic goals."[209] And the catalog actually included a smiley face.

At the March 23, 1996, meeting of the alumni association, the agenda was to set goals for the next five years and to discuss an affiliation with University of Maine at Nasson. Location—Leedy's restaurant in Alfred, Maine. There was no place on campus where alumni could meet.[210]

Still, alumni kept at it. On Saturday, October 19, 1996, the Nasson College Class of 1971 held its twenty-fifth reunion at the Port Gardens Restaurant and Inn, in Kennebunkport, Maine. "Our College May Be Gone … But We Party On," the flyer read. Some things never change.

At this point, what was left of Nasson College was minimal. There were rumors, there were facts, and there was no way to tell the two apart. Little hope that Nasson alumni would ever be able to establish any kind of permanent home remained. The Little Theatre was about to be demolished, but it wasn't. Allen Hall was rumored to have been used by federal agents for live fire training, but it wasn't. The dining commons was about to be torn down, and eventually it would be, but not then. At one alumni gathering on campus, alumni were told that what remained of Nasson College's records had been stored—piled on, thrown in—in the dining commons. With the commons about to be torn down, the alumni had to retrieve anything and everything they could, or it would all end up in a Dumpster, in the trash, in a landfill. Everyone grabbed yearbooks and anything that looked like it might have any historical or sentimental value. There was no place to leave it. Take it home. Take as much as you can. All that was left was trashed. And then there was nothing.

And things were about to get worse.

---

208 Catalog of Sanford Center, Summer 1996.
209 Ibid.
210 NCAA postcard.

THE SECOND AUCTION: 1996

RECALL THAT, WHEN MATTAR took over Nasson in 1984, the US Department of Education (ED) agreed to reduce the principal balance of the college loans. ED also granted Nasson College an eighteen-month moratorium (from March 1985 to September 1986) on making any payments.[211] However, after the moratorium on payments ended, Nasson College still failed to make a single payment under the new loan agreement. By fall 1994, all available methods of inducing the college to repay its loans had been exhausted, and ED began the foreclosure process.

In response, in 1995, Sanford's town treasurer Mike Ralston and Allen Mapes, together with staff from Senator William Cohen's office, went to Washington to meet with ED officials to discuss the status of the college loans. The group explained to ED that town property was landlocked by the Nasson properties and expressed the town's desire to take possession of the Nasson properties. The group offered to buy the properties for one dollar. The Department of Education declined the offer.[212] The Maine group then said that private investors were talking about putting a group together in order to make an offer for the properties. Soon after this meeting, officials from ED traveled to Springvale to inspect the properties in question—Marland Hall, Allen Hall, and the Science Center. ED's inspectors found the buildings to be in disrepair and in need of extensive renovation. During that visit, ED's representatives met with town officials, including the town administrator, town treasurer, and town counsel, who

---

211 US ED, "Inspector General."
212 Ibid.

expressed an interest in revitalizing the campus. However, they made it clear that the town was not able to purchase the buildings.

ED scheduled an auction for March 19, 1996. The department selected Keenan Auction Company to handle the sale. William Dale, attorney for the town of Sanford, sent a letter to ED stating that the town would be unable to actively participate in the auction. The town wanted to discuss the disposition of the properties and suggested that ED would receive no bids on the properties because they had a "negative value."

He was wrong.

As scheduled, an auction was held on March 19. ED received bids of $86,000 from Ken Ray for the science building and $47,000 from the Springvale Library for Allen Hall. No one bid on Marland Hall, so ED was forced to bid on this building "in house"; that is, the department had to bid on and purchase the property itself. There were reasons Dale had said the properties had negative value. The Science Center needed about $1 million to replace the electrical system, remove asbestos, and make the building ADA compliant. In addition, there was $6,200 in back taxes owed to the town. Allen Hall was to be demolished, so at least no repair costs were involved.[213]

All bidders were told that their deposits would be held, pending the outcome of a decision by the Supreme Judicial Court of Maine regarding the validity of the auction.

Indeed. Mattar sued ED, challenging the legalities of the foreclosure and the auction. Mattar alleged that ED, through its foreclosure action, was attempting to avoid the requirements of the federal law for the federal government to first make property available to agencies serving the homeless. In addition, Mattar alleged that unnamed ED officials had promised not to foreclose on the loan.

Mattar was referring to the McKinney Act, which concerned making housing available to the homeless.[214] However, the Department of Education determined that the act was not applicable to the college properties.[215] As for the supposed promises not to foreclose, there was no evidence to support Mattar's claims.

But that did not end the matter. In May 1996, the Superior Court

---

213 Mark Shanahan, "Two Nasson Buildings Are Sold Off in Auction," *Portland Press Herald*, March 20, 1996.

214 The McKinney–Vento Homeless Assistance Act of 1987 (Pub. L. 100-77, July 22, 1987, 101 Stat. 482, 42 U.S.C. § 11301 et seq.) is a United States law that provides federal money for homeless shelter programs. It was passed and signed into law on July 22, 1987.

215 US ED, "Inspector General."

of Maine set aside the March 1996 auction on the grounds that Nasson College had not received proper legal notice. The entire foreclosure process had to begin all over again. The new auction date was set for December 2, 1997, and was again scheduled to be conducted by Keenan Auction Company.[216]

More backstory—after (new) Nasson College lost its charter, the town of Sanford rezoned the college campus from nonprofit to commercial land and began assessing taxes. Nasson never paid any taxes. At the time of the second auction, Nasson was in arrears for back taxes of $11,000. ED asked town officials to waive the tax liability on these buildings to prevent ED from incurring additional expenses. By letter dated February 7, 1997, the town refused to waive the tax liability. Consequently, ED paid the overdue taxes in order to preserve its right to foreclose. Town treasurer Mike Ralston said that the town wanted ED to pay the taxes in order to save the town from incurring the legal costs to foreclose on the property. However, in a letter dated February 6, 1997, Allen Mapes asked ED not to pay the back taxes on the two dormitories, so that the town could foreclose and demolish the buildings to provide more parking in the area. It is not clear whether Ralston or Mapes knew what the other was suggesting. In any event, at no time did the town express any intention of buying the buildings.

The town also recognized that, as Theo Holtwijk, the town planner expressed, it was not in the real estate development business.[217] To resolve this issue, the town established the Sanford-Springvale Development Corporation (SSDC). The corporation would be composed of private citizens and public officials. Its mission was to handle the property on behalf of the town and to "do whatever is necessary to fill the building with tenants."[218]

They would have to wait for the next auction.

---

216 Ibid.
217 Mark Shanahan, "Sanford Proposal Would Market Old College Library 'Aggressively'," *Portland Press Herald*, May 28, 1996.
218 Ibid.

5

UNE COMES TO THE RESCUE

ONCE AGAIN, THE UNIVERSITY of New England entered Nasson's story.[219]
On October 21, 1996, John Downing, Nasson College Class of '59, wrote
to Elaine Bean, then president of the NCAA. Downing related that the
previous day he had presented to the UNE trustees the idea of "adopting"
the Nasson College Alumni Association into the "family" of UNE.[220]

Nasson alumni met with UNE officials to discuss the idea. UNE had
been through this before, having merged, in various ways, with St. Francis
College and Westbrook College. The trustees gave unanimous support to
explore the adoption process. Downing hoped that details could be worked
out quickly and a final plan presented to UNE on January 25, 1997.

That date was too ambitious, but the idea was pursued. A meeting
was planned for January 10 with the president of UNE and others.
Involved in the meetings and behind the scenes for Nasson were President
Elaine Bean, Meg Hutchins, Dave Plocharczyk, Robert Stone, and Rick
Schneider. Schneider drafted a proposed agreement between UNE and
the NCAA. Provisions of the suggested agreement were that UNE would
provide staff and operations to support the NCAA. The university would
publish an alumni update at least once a year. UNE would pay its own
expenses incurred in furtherance of the agreement and would help with
reunion planning, training for alumni leaders, and support for regional

---

219 In the final few years before Nasson College closed in 1983, Nasson and the
University of New England, which was also having some difficulties at the time,
had numerous discussions about merging the two schools or campuses. Nothing
lasting ever came out of those discussions.
220 John Downing, letter to Elaine Bean, then president of the NCAA, October 21,
1996.

59

networks and events. It would also help promote the sale of Nasson logo wear and other items. Further, UNE would provide a dedicated space at the main UNE campus for a Nasson College museum and/or other ways of memorializing the Nasson name, such as by endowing a faculty chair or a lecture series. UNE would also recognize that the NCAA was the only organization with authority to speak on matters concerning Nasson College alumni relations. Finally, UNE would provide space for an NCAA page on the UNE website.

In return, the NCAA would encourage donations to UNE from NC alumni for various UNE programs and scholarships. The NCAA would permit UNE to use Nasson's mailing list for fund-raising and promotional purposes.

Under the proposed agreement, each party would continue its own activities, except as specifically provided in the agreement. Nothing in the agreement could be deemed to create a partnership between the parties or an adoption or absorption of one party into the other. Additional provisions were proposed to ensure the independence and protection of each organization.

If anyone had flashbacks to the consortium agreements between Nasson College and UNE back in the early 1980s, it wasn't discussed.

After the meeting with UNE officials in January, Bean reported that UNE seemed very flexible. The UNE president said they were doing this because she felt it was the right thing to do.[221] John Downing indicated he could get NCAA some seed money to get the relationship off the ground. (He gave no indication what NCAA needed that money for.) Still, no commitments were made at the meeting.

On May 17, 1997, Bean announced the proposed agreement with UNE to the alumni at large.

As ever, things seemed to work in slow motion. It was not until the September 2, 1997, letter to Nasson alumni that details of the proposed agreement with UNE were given to the alumni.[222] The details were not very specific, but Nasson alumni stood to gain storage space for its mailing list; a meeting place; office support; mailings under UNE's permit; and as the letter said, "a future!" Also in the letter were details of the upcoming homecoming, and a mention that the SSDC had offered the alumni association a space in the Anderson Learning Center.

Homecoming was scheduled for October 4, 1997. The annual meeting would be held from 2:00 to 3:00 p.m. on the "long vacant" second (top)

---

221 Elaine Bean, e-mail to author, January 24, 1997.
222 Nasson Alumni Association, letter to "Alumnus," September 2, 1997.

floor of the ALC. That evening, the homecoming dance would be held at Spectators Sports Bar on Route 4/236 in Sanford. Michelle Windsor, '81, and Mike Bray, '82, of Bray's Brew Pub and Eatery in Naples, Maine, catered. As was often the case, music was provided by Stoney of America Music Services. (Robert Stone, "Stoney," provided pro bono entertainment for many alumni functions over the years.) The next day a brunch would be held for alumni to meet UNE's president at its Biddeford campus.

THE ALUMNI ASSOCIATION GETS A HOME BASE

What happened on that Saturday meeting in the library were the biggest game changers for Nasson alumni since the school had closed.

President Bean and John Downing gave presentations on the idea of UNE taking on NC alumni relations. The alumni warmly received the idea and approved the plan.

And then Anna Ashley got up to speak.[223] Ashley, class of 1960, told the alumni that the Sanford-Springvale Development Corp., which now controlled the Anderson Learning Center, had offered NCAA a space in the lower level of the ALC at a rent of one dollar per year.[224] In one instant, Nasson alumni suddenly had a home. It had a place to store its historical records and memorabilia.[225] Its officials had an office in which to do their jobs.[226] For the first time since the closing, Nasson alumni had a

---

223 Frederick St. Cyr, representing SSDC, also contributed to the presentation.

224 The space at that time was virtually uninhabitable. There was no electricity on the lower level, and there apparently had been floods, so the floor was covered in mud, and there was mold everywhere. Cinder block walls had to be taken down to combine rooms, and all the debris had to be hand carried out. While the cost of converting the space had been estimated at $40,000, extensive volunteer efforts brought the cost down to about $10 thousand. In a cooperative arrangement with the SSDC, the alumni center would also be used as a conference room for the Business Enterprise Center.

225 The ultimate historic memento is the portrait of George Nasson, founder of Nasson College. After the school closed in 1983, the Springvale Library obtained it. Following negotiations between Anna Ashley and Harland Eastman, a member of the library board, the portrait was sent to the Heritage Center. Lee Burnett, "Nasson's Traveling Show: Shuttle Diplomacy on Exhibit," *Journal Tribune*, May 6, 1998.

226 Ann C. Fisher, "Nasson Alumni Are Really Coming Home," *Sanford News*, September 23, 1997. The need for such a place was first raised by Victor DiGregorio at an alumni council meeting in 1983. He moved "to establish a committee to find a piece of property or building to house any and all Alumni and College memorabilia, and which will act as a catalyst to keep Nasson College alive." The motion was

new, permanent place on campus to meet and greet. All of the benefits that would have come from the UNE adoption were no longer needed. While there had been reluctant support for the UNE arrangement, emotions soared with news of the new home. John Downing was left with little to show for all his hard work,[227] but he too recognized that this was a better opportunity for the alumni.

The other big development was the maturation of the alumni website. At the time, the World Wide Web was pretty much brand new to the general public. Schneider had taken on the creation of a Nasson website as a personal project. The site, with its very unwieldy URL, http://members. aol.com/rschnei703/Nasson/default.htm, went online in early 1997. (The URL changed to a more manageable www.Nasson.org in September 1998.) The first version in those early Internet days was a primitive, single web page. But before too long, Schneider learned how to add additional pages and even photos and graphics! The site grew quickly. There was information on the history of the college, the alumni association, reunions, favorite memories, and an alumni directory, which has since grown to hundreds of names.[228] A visitor counter was added in June 1997. That month, there were 37 visits recorded. Sixty-five more in July, 149 in September, and 200 in October.[229] Nasson alumni who typed "Nasson College" into a search engine were startled and thrilled to discover that there really was life left at Nasson. By June 1999, there were 112 web pages of information on the site.

Now the rest of the UNE benefits were irrelevant. Nasson had its own home and website and a way to communicate with its alumni. The website recorded 1,000 hits by March 1998. By the end of 1998, 5,264 visitors had viewed the site. And on June 3, 1999, the site reached its 10,000th visitor. There were more than 11,000 hits in 1999 alone.[230]

The alumni association was granted 501(c)(3) tax-exempt status, meaning contributions to the association would be tax deductible.

---

seconded and passed unanimously ("Minutes of the Alumni Council," April 30, 1983.

227 The idea was not officially killed until a year later. Minutes for the annual meeting for October 3, 1998, contain this item: "The Board of Directors recommends to the general membership that the Nasson College Alumni Association politely withdraw from negotiations for affiliation with the University of New England because the Association has reestablished itself here in Springvale."

228 Alumni trivia: the first four alumni to be listed in the directory were (in class order) Rick Schneider, Connie Witherby, Elaine Bean, and Meg Hutchins, February 8, 1997.

229 Web page printouts in the author's collection.

230 The technical records do not distinguish between visits, page views, and the like.

And there was still a lot happening in Springvale. Mattar sold Brown Hall to Rob Reinken, who planned to turn the building into professional office space.[231] Alumni Hall had already been converted into apartments.

With the 1996 auction voided, Mattar still owned or controlled the gym, the dining commons, the Science Center, Allen Hall, and Marland Hall, so the fate of those campus buildings was still unresolved.

The good news was about to hit a wall.

---

231 "Brown Hall to Be Purchased, Renovated into Office Space," *Sanford News*, October 1997.

Nasson College
Springvale, Maine

Suggested Tour Route

- 9 Allen Hall
- 3 Alumni Hall
- 5 Anderson Learning Center
- 6 Art Gallery
- 34 Bradford Building
- 2 Brown Hall
- 13 Carriage House Art Studio
- 4 Coffee House
- 14 Dining Commons
- 7 Folsom Hall I
- 15 Folsom Hall II
- 16 Gliddon Hall
- 17 Grove Hall
- 18 Hanson Cottage
- 19 Home Management House
- 20 Holmes Hall
- 12 Huse Chapel
- 21 Infirmary
- 8 Lion's Den
- 11 Little Theater
- 22 Maine Hall
- 23 Marland Hall
- 24 Memorial Student Activity Center
- 25 Mitchell House
- 26 Oak Hall
- 27 President's House
- 28 Pryne-Husars Halls
- 29 Reed Hall
- 30 Ridley House
- 1 Science Building
- 31 Seminar Building
- 10 The Bookstore
- 32 Upper Campus I
- 33 Upper Campus II

Optional
- Reed Hall
- Art Studio
- Upper Campus

a. The college campus as it appeared in the early 1970s.

The Anderson Learning Center (library) is top center; Marland Hall and Allen Hall are on the right side. The dining commons and the gym are at bottom center, with the Little Theatre below the gym. Brown Hall and Alumni Hall are to the left of the gym, with the Science Center above them. The grassy quad is in the middle.

NASSON COLLEGE

SPRINGVALE, MAINE

VERITE PEUR

SANS

Seventy-Fifth

Commencement

August 12, 1989

b. Nasson College's 75th Commencement, 1989.
Brought to you by Edward Mattar III.

c. Brown Hall in ruins, 1997.

d. The Little Theatre in ruins, 1999.

e. The gym in ruins, 2002.

f. The campus "quad" on the eve of destruction.

The large building on the left is Allen Hall, and the dining commons flanks the tree at the rear. The gym is on the right.

g. The campus "quad" after demolition of
Allen Hall and the dining commons.

The four white panels are the side of the gymnasium. To the left,
not visible behind the trees, is the Springvale Public Library.

h. The Little Theatre was stabilized in late 1999.

i. Brown Hall was rescued and restored in 2000.

j. The newly restored and reopened gym
was home to youth basketball.

k. The Nasson College Alumni Flag Plaza.

College
Store

(For a detailed table of contents, and more information about this site, go to the Search page.)

Search

You are visitor number

[×]

since June 1997.

For technical information about this site, contact the webmaster (click here.)

Entire contents Copyright © 1997-2000. All Rights Reserved. (No copyright is claimed for federal or state publications, or for publications where the source is specifically identified.)

Old Fashioned Homecoming Parade Planned for October!

On Alumni Day on May 6th, the Association announced plans for next October's Homecoming Day. The morning will begin with coffee and donuts in the Heritage Center, as people register and revisit the Center.

Kicking off promptly at 12:00 noon will be an old fashioned Homecoming Parade up main street.

The scene from an old parade. The street looks a little different today, but otherwise it will be about the same. More or less.

While in years past, the parade went east on Main Street towards Shaw Field, this year the parade will travel west on Main Street, leading to Holdsworth Park, barely a ten minute walk from campus.

At Holdsworth Park, there will be the annual meeting of the Alumni Association, with a picnic -- hot dogs, hamburgers -- and much more. More details will be announced later.

The plan is for the parade to start at campus, picking up Oak Street, then turning left onto Main Street in Springvale. The spot for your photo op - "Kodak moment" will be to stand on the north side of the street, facing the campus: Bradford Block, Little Theatre and Seminar Building.

NOW IS THE TIME to start planning your place in the parade. Gather your friends / classmates / dorm

I. The alumni website kept alumni up-to-date on alumni activities, as well as chronicling what was happening on campus.

m. Alumni march in their homecoming parade, 2004.

These buildings on Main Street in Springvale have been there for more than one hundred years.

n. Last view of the quad before the grass was
torn up and parking lots were installed.

On the left is the gym, and on the right is Alumni Hall.

o. Installation of the parking lot.

To the right is the gym and to the left, under
construction, is the new courthouse.

p. Graduation in the gym in 2012—the Seacoast Career Schools.

q. The alumni association celebrated the grand opening of its new home, the Nasson Heritage Center in 1998.

Alumni President Elaine Bean and Heritage Center Chairman Anna Ashley.

r. Brown Hall in 2007, beautifully restored,
and looking better than ever.

s. The Little Theatre at Nasson restored, with a
lovely entranceway from Main Street.

t. The campus in 2012.

At top center is the Anderson Learning Center (the old college library). To its right is Marland Hall, and just below that is the new York County Career Center on Bodwell Court. Along Main Street, right to left, is the Springvale Public Library, the new courthouse, the old Seminar Building, the Bradford Block, and the Dennett Building. On the lower left corner is Key Bank. The large building above the Seminar Building is the Nasson Community Center (the gym and theater). The two buildings to the left of the NCC are Alumni Hall (apartments) and Brown Hall (offices). Above those two buildings, with the square and diamond, is the Science Center. Above the Science Center, to the left of the ALC is the former President's House, with Reed Hall attached. In the center, what used to be a grassy quad, is a parking lot. Compare with map on page 80. Now demolished is Allen Hall and the dining commons.

THE THIRD AUCTION: 1997

On October 16, 1997, Edward Mattar made a secret offer to buy Allen Hall, Marland Hall, and the Science Center from the Department of Education for $146,300, which was 10 percent more than the total bids from the 1996 auction. ED refused this offer, as it was not enough to cover the expenses ED had incurred since the that auction. ED then contacted Keenan Auction Company to find out if any other parties had expressed an interest in buying the buildings at auction. Keenan reported that it had spoken with the town administrator, who said that the town would not bid at the new auction, although town officials did plan to attend. Keenan reported back to ED that there was very little interest in the properties.

On October 29, 1997, ED made a counteroffer to Mattar; the department would sell him the buildings for $197,000. He declined the offer. Instead, on November 5, 1997, Bruce Read, attorney for a company called Effective Management Systems Inc. (EMS), made a written offer to purchase ED's interest in the buildings for $163,000, on the condition that the deal must be concluded by November 19, 1997. This offer was enough to cover expenses ED had incurred on the properties. On November 10, ED accepted EMS's offer for the mortgage notes on the Nasson properties. There was one other thing. Read asked Keenan Auction Company to keep the deal confidential. Keenan agreed and so did not tell town officials about the sale.

A spokesperson for ED later said that Keenan Auction Company had told the department it might not get even the $163,500 if an open auction were held.[232] But bidders from the previous auction argued that Keenan

---

232 Mark Shanahan, "Handling of Nasson Sale Ignites Backlash," *Portland Press Herald,*

had never talked to them to see if they were interested in bidding a second time.[233] Keenan insisted that there had been some discussions with the parties involved. Specifically, a real estate broker representing Ken Ray had been contacted. Ray denied that.[234] Ray, the successful bidder for the Science Center at the earlier auction, said he was considering bidding again for the building. Similarly, the Springvale Library said it was still interested in buying Allen Hall.[235] In any event, as one person pointed out, before an auction, you would never reveal how much you might bid, as it would reveal too much to competitors.

As a result of the secrecy, and in spite of the fact that the deal between EMS and ED precluded the *need* for an auction, Keenan held an open house as scheduled on November 18, 1997. Seven people attended. The open house had to be held in order for ED to preserve its ability to hold the auction on December 2, 1997, in case the transaction with EMS fell through. On November 24, 1997, the Department of Education and Effective Management Systems Inc. finalized the sale. By reacquiring the property at a discount, EMS washed away the debt to ED and eliminated most liens against the property.

The president, secretary, and treasurer of Effective Management Systems Inc., was Ed Mattar.

On the morning of the auction, fifty community boosters who had hoped the auction would free the buildings from neglect watched in disgust and humiliation as the auction turned into a power play by Mattar.

EMS, not ED, now owned the properties. EMS proceeded with the auction, but with a different auctioneer. Mattar sent Kennebunk attorney Alan Shepard as his agent. Numerous bidders remained, including Ken Ray, Robert Reinken, and Lionel Sevigny.[236] Ray again bid on the science building, Allen Mapes bid on Marland Hall, and others bid as well. Sevigny said he would have bid up to $200,000 for the Science Center if Mattar had not been in the picture.[237] The total bids from the local developers were more than ED had accepted from Mattar on the dubious advice

---

December 4, 1997.

233 Mark Shanahan, "Government Says It Was Told to Jump at Low Nasson Offer," *Portland Press Herald*, December 5, 1997.

234 Ibid.

235 Mark Shanahan, "Bids Expected for Nasson Buildings," *Portland Press Herald*, November 29, 1997.

236 Mark Shanahan, "Defaulter Buys Back Buildings at Nasson," *Portland Press Herald*, December 3, 1997.

237 Mark Shanahan, "Handling of Nasson Sale Ignites Backlash," *Journal Tribune*, December 4, 1997.

that no one might bid at all. The final bids were $115,000 for Marland Hall, $40,000 for Allen Hall, and $170,000 for the Science Center. EMS entered the final winning bids for each property and obtained clear titles. The $325,000 total was almost twice the $128,000 that the buildings had gotten in the March 1996 auction and much more than ED had just sold them for to EMS.[238]

By going through the motions of an auction, most old liens were wiped out. But since *the buyer and the seller were the same*—Mattar—no money had to change hands. No matter how high the public bids were, Mattar could outbid them, because he was only paying himself for the properties.

The place went nuts.

It took only one day for elected officials to get involved. Both Senator Olympia Snowe and Congressman Tom Allen said the people of Maine and all taxpayers deserved to know why the federal Department of Education had sold the properties to Mattar, when he still owed the department hundreds of thousands of dollars. State Senator Bruce MacKinnon of Sanford and State Senator James Libby[239] of Buxton also questioned the sale.[240]

Congressman Tom Allen said that he shared concerns about the Department of Education's decision to sell the buildings to Mattar. In Allen's view, ED's acceptance of Mattar's bid of $163,500 for the buildings without notifying local interested parties had not minimized the loss to taxpayers.[241] Allen said that, if there was any way to reverse the sale, he would try to do so.[242]

Allen contacted US Secretary of Education Richard Riley. Riley's response was that the department and its representatives acted in line with proper procedures. The department claimed that Sanford officials had told them that the town would not bid on the properties. Furthermore, because *Mattar had never assumed personal responsibility* for the debts previously incurred by Nasson College, nothing in the law prohibited him from purchasing the buildings. Allen said he had asked ED's inspector general to fully investigate the department's actions. Allen also noted that he had become aware that there were questions about the possible mishandling of student loan refunds at various institutions with which Mattar had been

238 Lee Burnett, "Mattar Deal Angers Community," *Journal Tribune*, December 3, 1997.
239 Libby is a Nasson College alumnus, class of 1983.
240 "Sale Ignites Backlash," *Portland Press Herald*, December 4, 1997.
241 Tom Allen, congressman, letter to Mike Walker, February 10, 1998.
242 Shanahan, "Handling of Nasson."

associated. He said ED had assured him the department continuing to take proper actions regarding those institutions.

Senator Snowe also sent letters to the secretary of education. On December 22, 1997, the department told Snowe that Nasson College, not Mattar personally, owed ED the mortgage money.[243]

Snowe noted that, while she had received a reply to her correspondence with the department over the Nasson situation, the agency's letter was not responsive to some of the issues she had raised.[244] Snowe asked the department to explore every legal option available to rescind the transfer of the property to Effective Management Systems and to reschedule a legitimate auction in which all interested bidders could compete. As Snowe said, "The whole episode is bizarre and makes no sense. How can someone who failed to pay all that money reap a reward for his bad behavior? It's beyond belief."[245]

The Finance Authority of Maine (FAME) also criticized the sale of the properties to Mattar.[246] It tried to pressure the federal government to restrict Mattar's access to federal student loans at a Rhode Island business training school. The school—called Nasson Institute—was already in danger of losing eligibility to participate in the federal student loan program.[247]

To be sure, there were some oddities about the transactions. For example, ED said that it allowed Mattar to exercise his "right of redemption" under Maine state law following foreclosure and before any auction. According to ED, the expiration of the redemption period was October 20, 1997; but the deal between Mattar and ED was not made until November 5, 1997. Thus, if there was no purchase completed by October 20, the right of redemption would have expired. So what authority did the department have to sell the properties prior to the scheduled auction?[248] ED then explained that Mattar did *not* obtain the properties under his redemption rights. Rather, he simply bought the properties directly from the department, as anyone else could have done.[249] Of course, it was ED that first raised the excuse

---

243 David Longanecker, assistant secretary, US ED, letter to Senator Olympia Snowe, December 22, 1997.

244 Olympia Snowe, senator, letter to Richard Riley, December 23, 1997.

245 Shanahan, "Government Says."

246 "Fame Joins Outcry Over Building Sales," *Portland Press Herald*, December 10, 1997.

247 Nasson Institute was reported to have three schools in Rhode Island. Its student default rate of 42.1 percent was nearly four times the national average of 10.4 percent. While the name of the schools is more than coincidental, there is no known corporate relationship with Springvale's Nasson.

248 Richard Schneider, letter to Congressman Tom Allen, January 5, 1998.

249 Mark Shanahan, "Government Says It Was Told to Jump at Low Nasson Offer,

of redemption in its letter of December 22, 1997 to Senator Snowe.[250] But with that second explanation, the whole redemption argument fell apart from the very beginning. If ED's argument was that it was Nasson College that owed the money and not Mattar, then it was only Nasson College that could have redeemed it, and Mattar never had any right of redemption at all.

On December 9, 1997, Schneider made a freedom of information request to the Department of Education.[251] He sought an exhaustive list of documents from the department:

1. All documents concerning the status of the Nasson College campus vis-à-vis the US Department of Education during the period 1982–1985 (in other words, up to the time the properties were conveyed to Edward Mattar).

2. All documents concerning the conveyance of the Nasson College properties to Edward Mattar, circa 1984–1985.

3. Any documents reflecting a purported agreement between the Department of Education or any representative of the department and Mattar concerning an alleged agreement by the department not to foreclose on Mattar should he fail to make payments on the properties.

4. All communications between the department and Mattar concerning Mattar's alleged failure to pay (in whole or in part) for the properties, including any communications or other documents reflecting compromise or forgiveness of the debt.

5. All documents concerning the decision to place the properties for auction around March 1996.

6. All documents concerning the decision to put the properties up for auction in December 1997.

7. All communications between the department and Effective Management Systems, a Nevada corporation believed to list Mattar as both president and clerk with the Nevada secretary of state.

Journal Tribune," December 5, 1997.

250 David Longanecker, assistant secretary, US ED, letter to Senator Olympia Snowe, December 22, 1997.

251 Apparently a Sanford attorney also made a FOIA request to the department, though the contents of that request are not known. (Julian Haines of Senator Susan Collins's office, e-mail to Richard Schneider, December 15, 1997.)

8. All documents showing whether and how Mattar had (or had not) actually paid for the buildings purchased from the department in November 1997.

9. All communications between the department and Keenan Auction Company of Portland, Maine, concerning the Nasson College campus buildings.

10. Any other documents in the department's possession concerning the Keenan Auction Company of Portland, Maine.

11. All communications between the department and Murphy Auction Company of Kennebunk, Maine, concerning the Nasson College campus buildings.

12. Any other documents in the department's possession concerning the Murphy Auction Company of Kennebunk, Maine.

13. All documents reflecting Mattar and/or the Career Institute and an alleged failure to reimburse the department for student loans.

14. All documents relating to Mattar and the "Nasson Institute," believed to be located in Pawtucket, Rhode Island, and an alleged failure to reimburse the department for student loans.

15. All documents relating to Mattar and Nasson University, believed to be located in Mobile, Alabama, and an alleged failure to reimburse the department for student loans.[252]

Schneider also asked for a waiver of all search and duplication fees.

It's a good thing he asked for that waiver, because the department told him they had found approximately 3,500 pages of relevant materials. The costs were to include a $200 search fee, and an $800 copying fee.[253] Schneider again asked for a waiver, arguing that provision of the materials was in the public interest and not any commercial interest. The department denied the waiver.

Then Senator Collins got involved. She sent a letter to the secretary of education asking for reconsideration of its decision to charge the NCAA (acting through Schneider) for search and duplication fees.[254] Collins made

---

252 Richard Schneider, letter to the Department of Education, December 9, 1997.
253 There were various adjustments to the basic costs; for example, the first one hundred pages were free.
254 Susan Collins, senator, letter to US ED Secretary Richard Riley, March 9, 1998.

the point that the secretary should use his discretion to waive the fees. As Collins explained, "The many people of Maine who have felt the impact of this sale either directly or indirectly have legitimate concerns over the conduct of the transaction. From their perspective the sale was shrouded in mystery, and was orchestrated from Washington, with no regard to the interest of the local community. ... In this instance, the disclosure would not only make ... a contribution, it would help restore people's faith in the open function of the federal government." Collins then suggested that costs might be minimized if a representative of the alumni association went to the department to inspect the materials and designate for copying only those documents deemed most important.

It took a while and a lot of communications from members of Congress—Congressman Allen and Senator Snowe also got involved—but ED finally allowed a representative of the alumni association, Schneider, to review the documents, select the most important materials, and have them copied at no charge.[255] Schneider eventually spent most of one day going through some 8,000 pages (somehow it had grown from the original estimate of 3,500 pages) of materials, and marked for copying a couple of hundred pages. At that point, the reproduction of the materials was actually in response to a request from Senator Collins, not Schneider's original FOIA request. It was a kind of compromise—a way for ED to save face, avoid the statute requiring fees to be paid, and be responsive to a member of Congress. The materials were sent directly to Collins's office, where Schneider picked them up.

So after all that, what was in the material Schneider had selected? Any smoking guns? No, just evidence of a huge mess—actions and decisions that were not carefully considered throughout the fifteen or so years since Mattar came on the scene.

In the meantime, ED issued a three-page letter of explanation about the sale. According to Assistant Secretary of Education David Longanecker, the decision to sell the buildings to Mattar was "consistent with the department's obligation to minimize loss to the taxpayers."[256] The letter seemed to satisfy no one, and Senator Collins and Representative Allen both called for an investigation of the sale by the ED inspector general. Still, Longanecker conceded, "In hindsight, it might have been helpful

---

255 Donald Rappaport, letter to Senator Susan Collins, April 2, 1998.
256 David Longanecker, Assistant Secretary, US ED, letter to Senator Olympia Snowe, December 22, 1997, as reported in Mark Shanahan, "Education Official Defends Sale of Nasson Buildings to Mattar," *Portland Press Herald*, December 23, 1997.

to have given advance notice to town officials of the intent to accept Mr. Mattar's final offer."[257]

On May 7, 1998, the Department of Education inspector general issued his report on the sale of the Nasson College properties in 1997. The IG concluded:

> The Department of Education (ED) did not violate any laws when it sold its interest in Nasson College properties to Effective Management Systems Inc. on November 24, 1997. In addition, ED's actions, in the 1997 sale of its interest in the Nasson College properties, were reasonable to protect the Federal taxpayers' interests.
>
> Based on numerous interviews conducted and a review of documents and letters, the primary concern of Town of Sanford officials and citizens was ED's failure to notify the town of its intention to sell its interest in the Nasson College properties to Edward Mattar, former Chairman of the Board of Nasson College and President, Treasurer and Secretary of Effective Management Systems Inc., and the individual some believe incurred the debt. However, Nasson College borrowed $1,175,000 from ED and ceased payment on the debt before Mr. Mattar became involved with Nasson College. In 1985, as Chairman of the Board of Nasson College, Mr. Mattar convinced ED to reorganize the loans, which reduced the outstanding balance from approximately $826,000 to $400,000. Nasson College incurred the $400,000 debt, not Mr. Mattar.
>
> At the time of the transaction, ED's College Housing Facilities staff concluded that the offer from Effective Management Systems Inc. was the best option for Federal taxpayers. They based their decisions on letters, discussions, and prior actions by Sanford town officials, the marketing responses to the auction, and the physical deterioration of the properties.
>
> In October 1997, ED received an offer to buy its interest in Nasson College. At any time private investors, the town, or anyone could have approached ED with a similar option. However, none did. If a private investor or any entity had

---

257 Shanahan, "Education Official Defends."

bought the mortgage from ED, they would have had to clear the title to the property by holding an auction. This would have given Mr. Mattar the opportunity to obtain the property by making the highest bid, something he could have done if ED had held the second auction.

Under the HEA [Higher Education Act], 20 U.S.C., 1132d, ED has the authority to make loans to institutions of higher education for the construction of academic and educational facilities for students and faculty. It was under this program, or a predecessor to it, that Nasson College obtained a loan from ED to finance the construction of the three buildings at issue. This statute also provides ED with its own authority to foreclose on and dispose of such property. It gives ED the express authority to foreclose on and dispose of properties that serve as collateral on construction loans to institutions of higher education and imposes no procedural requirements for doing so. The statute specifically provides that no other provision of law relating to the disposition of real property applies to such property.

ED's actions regarding the transfer of its interest in the Nasson College properties were reasonable to protect the federal taxpayers' interest. The information available to ED before the second auction – including the Town of Sanford's statements that it would not purchase the property – made its decision to accept the offer of an amount that covered the Federal government's expenses reasonable. The realization that the auction would net few or no bids was based on the fact that the town counsel reported the property had a negative value, little marketing response had occurred, and the properties sat idle for an additional 20 months following the March 1996 auction.

Incredibly, the inspector general finished with this note:

Despite Mr. Mattar's problems with other schools, Mr. Mattar still has the ability to conduct business with ED and other government agencies. Even if he were debarred, which he is not, Mr. Mattar would not have become debarred from buying ED's interest in the Nasson College Properties.[258]

The bottom line—Mattar was back.

THE NASSON HERITAGE CENTER

The grand opening of what was to be named the Nasson Heritage Center was held the weekend of May 2, 1998. In attendance were thirty-five alumni; six faculty and staff of the old school; and many friends, relatives, townspeople, and invited guests. Marion Prosser, class of 1921, Nasson's senior alumna, went too. Robert "Stoney" Stone, '72, welcomed everyone to the center. A longtime Beatles fan, Stoney related to "Imagine," the old John Lennon song. "You may say I'm a dreamer ..." He said it was probably the first time in history that an alumni association had dedicated a new operation like this fifteen years after the school had closed.[259] He recognized Anna Ashley for being the prime mover in getting the center created. Stoney also thanked everyone else for making the center a reality.

Elaine Bean, president of the Nasson College Alumni Association, said she was overwhelmed by the new center. She said that, for the past fifteen years the alumni association had been like the famous "Man without a Country"—still alive, but with no permanent residence. She thanked Rick Schneider for putting the word out about the center on the alumni website and for keeping everyone up to date with frequent reports. Bean thanked Ashley; Meg Hutchins Broderick, '78; Robert Stone, '72; Ernie Nason, '75; Mike Bray, '82; Ann Fisher, '83; and Sally Hapenny, '57. She expressed the association's appreciation to the Sanford-Springvale Development Corporation for renting the space to the association. Anna Ashley then thanked everyone for all they had done to make the center a reality. She noted the many e-mails that kept everyone together and moving in the same direction. She thanked everyone for their encouragement and then asked everyone to send more money. [260]

Ashley read a letter from Maine's US Senator Susan Collins. Collins wrote:

> Please accept my warmest congratulations as you gather at the Anderson Learning Center to celebrate the opening of

---

258 US ED, "Inspector General."
259 As reported on www.Nasson.org\nca\opening. Accessed November 7, 2011.
260 Ibid.

the new Nasson Heritage Center. I regret that my schedule keeps me from joining you for this special occasion.

Everyone involved in the creation of the Nasson Heritage Center – from the Alumni Association to the Sanford-Springvale Development Corporation – should be very proud of their enduring commitment to the spirit of Nasson College and to the communities of Sanford-Springvale. Thanks to your hard work and dedication, the history of a fine college will be preserved and displayed. Perhaps more important, the Nasson Alumni Association and other community groups will have a place to meet, to renew friendships, and to plan other local projects.[261]

One of the things that kept the Nasson.org website so lively at that time was the constant reporting of news. Schneider designed the website as if the school were still open, rather than simply reporting on reunions and past events. Of course, there were no pages on the application process or registering for classes, but current events always found their way to the front page. In fact, during this time so much was happening on and to the campus that Schneider had front-page headlines backed up for days at a time. He knew that, unlike the daily newspaper, most people did not visit the website every day, so he wanted to leave news up front for a least a few days at a time. As a result, alumni and others had a reason to frequently visit the website to see what was happening. In March 1999, there were 1,120 visits to the site.

Another old loose end unexpectedly appeared. It seemed that the original George Nasson Trust fund, the one George Nasson himself had created in his will long before the original Nasson Institute opened in 1912, had always existed, independent of the school.[262] All throughout the existence of Nasson Institute, then Nasson College, the trust fund remained a unique entity, separate and apart from the school. Richard Ford revealed in late 1998 that Albert Prosser was the last trustee of the fund, and since he had recently died, the fund was in limbo. In response,

---

261 Susan Collins, senator, letter to Anna Ashley, April 30, 1998.

262 "I give, devise and bequeath unto Asa Low, Esq., Irving A. Butler, and Chas. H. Frost and to their successors, all the rest and remainder of my real estate, in trust for the following purposes ... to establish and maintain an Institute for the education of Young Ladies, to be known as the Nasson Institute, which shall be carried on to promote the moral, intellectual and physical instruction and education of young women." (George Nasson, will dated March 24, 1881.)

the NCAA proposed three new trustees for the fund,[263] Bill Hoag, Dick Ford, and Anna Ashley.[264] The association's attorney, Bob Ferguson, then made an application to the judge of probate. He argued that the fund, then containing about $32,000, should go to the NCAA.[265] The petition was granted, and the trust fund was turned over to college alumni. The new trustees had to go back to the court to modify the will so the association could assess the trust's interest for scholarships. The petition requested more flexibility in investments and requested that the NCAA supplant the defunct Nasson College as the beneficiary of the funds.[266] It seemed George Nasson's own trust fund had come home. The petition was granted.

With alumni in their new home in the ALC, activities picked up. The website was regularly reaching one thousand visitors a month, not bad for a school that only had a few thousand students in its entire history.[267] Homecoming 1998 included photo ops for class reunions, lunch, the association's annual meeting, and dinner and dancing on the third floor of the ALC.[268]

There arose the matter of some thirty to forty "graduates" with degrees (such as they were) from Mattar's Nasson College. After a difficult, sometimes tortuous discussion, the NCAA decided that Mattar's students would be accepted as Nasson alumni, eligible for participation in the NCAA, if they met the requirements set forth in the bylaws.[269] But only one or two ever made contact with the alumni association.

---

263 NCAA Board Meeting minutes, October 3, 1998.
264 NCAA Board Meeting minutes, February 20, 1999.
265 See NCAA Board Meeting minutes, November 14, 1998.
266 NCAA Board Meeting minutes, February 20, 1999.
267 Nasson website, home page, assessed January 30, 1998.
268 NCAA postcard and homecoming flyer.
269 NCAA Board Meeting minutes, February 20, 1999.

THE SPRINGVALE PUBLIC LIBRARY
COMES TO THE RESCUE

In 1998, the Springvale Public Library, housed in what once was a small, historic single-family house on Main Street in Springvale, was bequeathed $3.4 million by the late L. Orlo Williams, a lawyer who served on the library's board of trustees for decades.[270] The library was a community institution in Springvale, with a collection of some thirty thousand books. Its budget of about $100,000 a year came almost entirely from town funds.

C. Scott Hoar, a selectman from Sanford, called Mattar. The call led to an in-person meeting at Heald Family Center between Mattar and a handful of people, including David Heald; Lionel Sevigny; Town Administrator Jack Webb; William Roberts, who was then the chairman of the board of selectmen; and others.[271] Negotiations continued throughout the year. Finally, on November 16, 1998, David Heald, president of the SSDC, announced that the corporation had negotiated the acquisition of two former Nasson properties from Mattar, on behalf of the Springvale Library Association.[272]

The deal was that, through SSDC, the library would purchase Allen Hall and the MSAC (the gym, the theater, and the dining commons) from

---

270 Gregory Kesich, "Group Buys Nasson Buildings," *Portland Press Herald*, November 17, 1998.

271 Lee Burnett, "Springvale Looks Ahead to New Era," *Journal Tribune*, November 17, 1998; Lee Burnett, "Heald Was the Right Negotiator for a Difficult Deal," *Journal Tribune*, November 17, 1998.

272 Press Release from SSDC (November 16, 1998).

Mattar for $300,000. The acquisition would finally enable the redevelopment of the old Nasson campus. A new Maine District Courthouse was planned, along with a major expansion of the Springvale Public Library. Both Allen Hall and the dining commons were to be demolished. The development team was composed of Hazen Carpenter, Lionel Sevigny, and Allen Mapes. Exactly why Mattar finally decided to sell out and give up all his interests in the campus was never known, but on November 16, 1998, the buildings were deeded to the Springvale Library, through the SSDC.

At last, Mattar was gone—totally and forever.

With the old campus properties now in the hands of local owners, campus redevelopment could finally get under way. Tearing down the old dining commons would create space for the new courthouse.[273] The state had $3 million to spend on it. Tearing down Allen Hall would allow for shared parking for the courthouse, the Anderson Learning Center (still owned by the town), and the public library. Also, with Allen Hall gone, the ALC would be visible from Main Street, making leasing space in the ALC easier. At the time, tenants of the ALC included the University of Maine, Sweetser Children's Services, SSDC, and the Nasson Heritage Center. Acquisition of the old gymnasium, which was attached to the dining commons but which was not to be torn down, could provide plenty of room for youth basketball programs, which were then using the cramped, old Springvale Town Hall.

Nearly two hundred alumni attended homecoming 1998. Elaine Bean stepped down after ten years as president of the alumni association and was succeeded by Richard Ford, '65.

The next year, homecoming 1999 included workshops on various topics designed to bring alumni up to date on recent events. Anna Ashley spoke of plans for the future of the campus. Rick Schneider talked about what had happened to the campus since the school closed in 1983. Dick Ford talked about fund-raising and the endowment campaign. Bill Hoag presented information on the new scholarship program. Natalie Hoag and Eugene Daly discussed the Heritage Center. Over two thousand active names appeared on the official mailing list.[274]

---

273 Ellen W. Todd, "Group Is Working to Locate Courthouse on Nasson Campus," *Sanford News*, October 8, 1998.
274 Dick Ford, "Notes from the President," *Nasson News* (Winter 2000), 2.

PLANS FOR OTHER CAMPUS BUILDINGS

There were plans for other campus buildings as well, including some that were never owned or controlled by Mattar.

For example, at the original auction in 1984, Dictar Associates had purchased the upper campus buildings, including Pryor-Hussey and the former New Division. The dorms and land totaled about nineteen acres.[275]

In May 1989, Sherman Baldwin and Michael Miles, two graduates of Nasson College, class of 1983, announced plans to convert the three upper campus buildings into a center for international communication and understanding, at a cost of some $4.5 million. They even met with alumni at the council's meeting on May 20, 1989. Of course, the first thing they needed to do was buy the property from Dictar Associates. The two said that, while they had already met once with a representative of Dictar, they were not yet close to a deal.[276] At the time, Dictar had an application before the Maine Housing Authority for funding to turn two upper campus buildings into apartments for low- and moderate-income families. The Baldwin/Miles plan never materialized.

Neither did Dictar's. Dictar eventually failed to meet the payments on its mortgage, so Maine National Bank took over the property. Then, in May 1991, the bank auctioned off the upper campus buildings once again, and this time they were purchased by John Perry. Perry paid $30,000, along with sewer and water fees that had accrued. His plan was to convert the buildings into affordable apartment housing. That plan never happened either.

Instead, in 1992, John Barth announced plans to open a school in the upper campus. He purchased Pryor-Hussey and both upper campus buildings for a reported $100,000.[277] Reaction to Barth's plans was positive in the community. Sanford selectmen called it "terrific," and said that an active school in Springvale would be a welcome addition.[278] As the *Journal Tribune* opined, "No one wants to see the upper campus continue on its slide toward decay. And no one wants to see a plan for saving the campus stop in its tracks because the impetus or the support simply wasn't

---

275 Mary Raitt Jordan, "Prep School Planned for Former Nasson Property," *Journal Tribune*, June 10, 1992. The auction year was reported as 1985.

276 C. Scott Hoar, "Nasson Upper Campus Plan Unveiled," *Portland Press Herald*, May 20, 1989.

277 Daniel O. Bellow, "A Different Effort Seeks to Plan Lenox School on Site in Maine," *Bershire Eagle*, 1992.

278 Editorial, "Hope for Renewed Life at a Slumbering College," *Journal Tribune*, June 13, 1992.

there. With hard work and money on Barth's part and encouragement and community support on the town's, maybe—just maybe—Nasson will rise again.[279]

Barth planned to create the Springvale School. He met with the alumni and explained that the new school would offer a college preparatory program for grades seven through twelve. It would be a coed, nonsectarian, residential school.[280] The school's program would emphasize community responsibility. First, it would develop a sense of public duty on the part of future professionals. Second, it would include a charitable program, with scholarships for qualified students. In addition, one of its programs would sponsor orphans in developing nations. Each student, through his or her tuition, would support an orphan in a foreign country.

The three buildings that would make up Springvale School were in need of major restoration work. Roofs had to be replaced, and underground oil tanks had to be dug out and removed. Interiors had been vandalized over the years, and the electrical systems had been ruined by water leaks. Built-in furniture was trashed, and in Fobes Hall (the original New Division, later Upper Campus I), the glorious copper fireplace hood was long gone. Barth said it would take years to complete the repairs to the buildings. But his plan was to grow slowly and carefully. He hoped to have something in operation beginning in 1999, possibly tutoring or a summer arts programs for adults. He would then add a nonresidential, academic summer school. Eventually, there was to be a year-round residential program.[281]

Sanford's purchase of the ALC was finally beginning to pay off. The town had spent $1.5 million since 1985 to buy and renovate the old library. But over the years, occupancy had risen, and rental income was finally covering the mortgage and other bills.[282] Tenants now included the University of Maine Sanford Center; Sweetser Children's Services Inc.; the Business Enterprise Center; the Southern Maine Regional Planning

279 Ibid.

280 Mark Shanahan, "'Dreamer' Sees School Rising from Ruins," *Maine Sunday Telegram*, August 25, 1996.

281 While renovation work continued over the years, as of 2011, the school had never opened for students.

282 Such is the nature of high finance: The mortgage on the library, in the amount of $131,000, was held by Key Bank when the town acquired the mortgage. The bonds were Academic Building Bonds of 1969. In 1995, Mellon Bank acquired bond services from Key Trust and assumed the mortgage. In 1997, Chase Manhattan Bank acquired the corporate trust business of Mellon and, as a result, assumed the mortgage. (Paula Simpson, [Sanford] Town Treasurer, memo to John Webb, [Sanford] Town Administrator, October 7, 1999.)

Commission; and the Nasson College Heritage Center. Sweetser announced that it would move up to the third floor and rent 3,000 square feet.

Allen Hall and the dining commons were finally demolished in May 1999. It took about ten days to take down the dining commons and only three days to take down Allen Hall.[283] The roof of the gym was beginning to leak, though the Little Theatre remained dry. Brown Hall had been a wreck, but it was finally renovated and reopened as an office building by Rob Reinken. Alumni Hall had long since been turned into an apartment house by Reinken. Marland Hall was saved but remained empty. The Science Center also remained empty and deteriorating. Both were now owned by Rob Reinken.

The Springvale Redevelopment Corporation (SRC) was created in 1998 as a subsidiary of the Springvale Public Library Association to manage and direct the rehabilitation of parts of the campus.[284] Officers of the SRC were Lionel Sevigny, Allen Mapes, and Hazen Carpenter. Among their tasks were to oversee hazardous waste removal, demolition, underground utilities and drainage, parking, and landscaping.[285] Among other major goals was the restoration of the gymnasium, which they estimated would cost $500,000. According to Mapes, Mattar had stripped the building—there remained no sprinkler system, no fire alarm system, and little emergency lighting. The roof needed replacing, most of the windows were broken, the maple wood floor was warped in one area, and the lockers and bleachers were gone. It needed a new boiler and was certainly not handicapped accessible. Still, SRC contended that there was a "gigantic need in town for this structurally sound building."[286]

Acquiring all the necessary land for a courthouse continued to be a challenge. Dennis Fortin, who owned the Seminar Building, agreed to sell some land to add street frontage to the proposed courthouse. The selling price was $30,000. This enabled new water and sewer connections to the gym and other buildings.[287] Part of the deal was that Fortin could have six designated parking places adjacent to the Little Theatre and six nondesignated parking spaces in the general parking area.[288]

By now, Rob Reinken had taken possession of the Science Center,

---

283 www.Nasson.org. Accessed May 31, 1999.
284 Allen Mapes, draft letter, describing the SRC (June 2, 1999); Minutes from SSDC Trustees Meeting, January 7, 1999.
285 Ibid.
286 Ibid.
287 Ibid.
288 Ibid.

Brown Hall, Alumni Hall, Marland Hall, and Folsom I and II.[289] His plans for Marland called for using that old dorm as a residential and congregate-care facility. He also built a small building on Bodwell Court, between Marland Hall and the site of old Allen Hall.[290] This would become the York County Career Center.

As the twentieth century drew to a close, it was apparent that, at long last, the future was now. And the old grassy quad in the center of campus, soon to be paved over into a parking lot, would henceforth be known as "Nasson Common."

---

289 NCAA Board Meeting minutes, February 20, 1999.

290 The building was built roughly on the site of old Bodwell Manor, which was originally a private residence, acquired by the college for use as a small dormitory before it was demolished in 1968.

ALUMNI ACTIVITIES SOAR

By 2000, THE NASSON College Alumni Association was active year round. Some would say the association was more active in 2000 than it was when the school was still open. In fact, there was so much going on that the Nasson College yearbook, the *Nugget*, was revived.

Of course, it wasn't the same. This *Nugget* had no class years, no sports, no dorms. Instead of reporting on a couple hundred students, there were only a couple score of alumni to report on. But the alumni were busy. The first of the revived yearbooks was for the "school year" 2000–2001 and was timed to be available at homecoming 2001. The yearbook reported on the association itself, with sections on the board, the administrative committee, homecoming and alumni day in the spring, and other activities. The association announced a new scholarship to be awarded each year (no, the recipient did not have to attend Nasson College), and there were full-page articles on the Heritage Center. Rick Schneider and Pete Smith began recording video histories of members of the Nasson family. That year, Schneider interviewed Nasson's senior alumna, Marion Prosser, of the class of 1921, as well as Marion Sugden, '32; Mary Elizabeth Beaton, '51; and George Gillis, '55.

The Internet became busier than ever. Added to the site were more historical documents, maps of the old campus, more directories of alumni, favorite memories, and lots of pictures of the campus, then and now. One of the popular features was the "Lion's Den," a web-based chat room in which people would gather online either impromptu or on a prearranged schedule to discuss news of the day and old times.

Eighteen years after Nasson closed and eighteen years after its very own radio station was stilled, Radio Nasson came back to life as an Internet production. Originally, WNCY-FM was a 10-watt FM radio station, the brainchild of H. Pete Smith, broadcasting from the third floor of Brown Hall and receivable throughout the Mousam River Valley. Thanks to the Lion's Den chat room, Smith and other alumni gave birth to that sound once again. Smith, Stoney, Rick Schneider, Joe Bartucca, Steve Bell, Savery Moore, Connie Witherby, Anna Ashley, Mark Lillie, and many others, gathered every Tuesday evening for months to map out plans, concepts, alternatives, costs, and production methods, in an effort to restore one of Nasson's most endearing and beloved activities.

While it was no longer possible to actually operate an FM radio station, the group instead designed a system to "broadcast" over the Internet. They pulled it off. "Web-NCY" went "on the air" on January 11, 2001,[291] and thereafter presented a half-hour program every two weeks.[292] Each program included "news" updates of campus and alumni activities, interviews with various alumni and others, and occasionally original music created by alumni. And because the station was web-based, each program remained on line, on demand for listening, 24/7, all over the world.[293]

The College Store was back in business. No textbooks were for sale, but most everything else a college bookstore might sell was represented. Under the administration of Janice Longfellow and her team, they offered a full selection of logo wear—T-shirts, sweatshirts, polo shirts, denim shirts, jackets, and barbeque aprons were all available in the college colors of maroon and gold, with the college seal emblazoned on each piece. Souvenirs? You could buy a coffee mug, a tote bag, a mouse pad, and a CD-ROM of old Nasson photos. Some books were available, including Prosser's history, each year's new yearbook, and books written by former Nasson College faculty and students.

The Nasson News grew bigger and became more active. Running about twelve tabloid-sized pages, the paper ran articles on all the current events of the association. Assisting Editor in Chief Connie Witherby, '73, were Senior Editor Anna Ashley, '60, and editors Natalie Hoag, '56, and Robert

---

291 Richard Schneider, e-mail to Pete Smith, January 11, 2001.

292 The program's name, "Web-NCY" was a play on the old radio station's official FM call letters, WNCY. Since the third floor of Brown Hall was never remodeled, the original radio station studios remain pretty much the same as the day the school closed in 1983, though without any equipment. Sadly, the old studios were not available for use by the new programmers.

293 That's not hype. A detailed analysis of web hits to www.Nasson.org revealed visitors from the United Kingdom, Canada, Singapore, Italy, Hong Kong, Australia, Israel, Sweden, India, Greece, and Indonesia. (Visitor analyses for March, May, and June, 1999.)

Stone, '72. Former English professor Leonard Whittier assisted with editing (of course). Contributors included Richard Ford, '65; Helen King Dostie, '59; Norman Pulaski, '62; Amy Stevenson Ross, '59; George Gillis, '55; June Gillis, '54; H. Pete Smith, '72; and former English professor Allen Scott. Contributing photographers included Rich Gardner, '75; Don Penta, '71; and Charlene Romanko Durmont, '60.

Reunions were not just all-inclusive gatherings each year. There were special group reunions too. The 2000–2001 year saw reunions for the class of 1951 (fifty years!); the study abroad program in Florence, Italy; and a Glidden Hall reunion for residents of that dorm from the class of 1974. There was even a regional reunion held in the Washington, DC, area.

On October 7, 2000, people in Springvale watched in amazement as the first Nasson homecoming parade in eighteen years made its way up Main Street. Historically, the parade would be a prelude to a soccer game at Shaw Field. The games were long gone, and Shaw Field was no longer part of the Nasson campus, but the parade itself could be recreated—kind of. Instead of traveling from downtown Springvale up the road to Shaw Field, this parade set off from the parking lot next to the Science Center, turned left onto Oak Street, then left again onto Main Street. The crowd marched up the road to Holdsworth Park, where everyone enjoyed lunch and other reunion festivities. A Sanford police cruiser led the way, blocking traffic on Main Street (much to the consternation of local residents).[294]

The next year, 2001, saw the old grass quad torn up so that a new parking lot could be built in its place. The new Springvale courthouse began construction on the site of the old dining commons parking lot.

Homecoming 2001 was the largest gathering of Nasson alumni to date. There were 230 registered participants. It was said that never before—not even when the school was still open—had 230 alumni attended homecoming.

The homecoming parade became a regular part of homecoming activities. Instead of marching to Holdsworth Park as alumni had done the previous year, the 2001 parade began behind the library on Bradeen Street, turned right onto Kirk Street, and then made another right onto Main Street. The old alumni marched past Springvale Auto Parts, Vic Remy's Market, Demer's Pharmacy, Western Auto, Down Maine House, Luigi's, Dairy Queen, Beland's Variety, and Normans (the stores were all gone, but they were visible at least in the parade marchers' minds). The alumni turned right again at the bank and then back onto Bradeen Street,

---

294 Stoney, "Homecoming 2000," 3, 6.

and the parade ended where it had begun just a few minutes before. No floats or costumes, but lots of enthusiasm.

Some years, there was actually a kind of a reviewing stand, with the parade being called by Rick Schneider and Stoney. Here's the order of the 2001 parade, along with the announcer's original commentary:

1. Our police escort, Sanford's Finest, the Sanford Police Department

2. An American Color Guard, brought to us by the Veterans of Foreign Wars

3. The Nasson College Alumni Association parade banner

4. In our first car, the president of the Nasson College Alumni Association, Richard G. Ford

5. Ladies and gentlemen, the senior alumna of Nasson College, Miss Marion Williams Prosser, Nasson Institute, class of 1921.[295]

6. Our entertainment for today, the pride of Sanford, the Sanford High School marching band – The band is under the direction of Matt Doiron. The assistant director is Majorie Olson. The percussion instructor is Frank Ricker. The color guard instructor is May E. Bailey. The Sanford High School band is a sixty-member marching band complete with color guard. Today, the band is playing ...[296]

7. The Mapes Oil Truck from 1926 – Note the original telephone number, 67W.

8. The famous original radio station banner for Nasson College radio, WNCY, carried this year by Judy Mallanik, Nasson College, class of 1972, and Heather McNiven King, also from the NC class of 1972.

9. And now, ladies and gentlemen, the alumni of Nasson College!

10. Finally, closing up our Nasson College Homecoming Parade for 2001, the Sanford-Springvale fire truck, Pumper Number 1.

---

295 Marion was celebrating her *eightieth* class reunion.
296 The announcer never did find out what that piece of music was.

For parade watchers, and there were always some, the parade looked different depending on where you stood. If you were on the campus side of Main Street, you were looking at a shopping mall. It had been decades since the Main Street businesses had been demolished. But if an onlooker stood on the *business* side of the street and looked *toward* campus, he or she took in a familiar sight. Still there were Brown Hall and Alumni Hall, The Dennett Building (site of Jo Emma's Jewelers), the Bradford Block, and what had once been the Seminar Building. In all these years, that view had hardly changed. [297]

The first alumni scholarships were awarded to children of alumni. Alumni of the Year Awards were given to Meg Hutchins Broderick, '78, and Rick Schneider, '71, for their distinguished service to the alumni association. Robert "Stoney" Stone" was presented with a Gold Key. He had received the award in 1983, along with an IOU for the then out-of-stock pin, as the college had closed, and now eighteen years later, he finally redeemed the latter.

During the year, Web-NCY presented live recordings from homecoming and a replay of a 1975 basketball game between Nasson and Thomas College, as called by then students Joe Bartucca and Savery Moore. The recorded history project continued with interviews of Morton Gold, Bud Johnston, H. Allen Mapes, Dean Edward Durnall, and Steve Morris.

And on the morning of April 8, 2002, alumni all over the country looked up from their breakfast cereal and did a double take. There, on national TV, was a Nasson College banner. June and George Gillis had managed to get in front of the crowd at Rockefeller Center in New York and actually made it onscreen with Al Roker, the *Today Show* weatherman; and waved the Nasson banner for all the world to see.

---

297 The Dennett building is the oldest building in Springvale Village, built about 1856. The Bradford Block was built about 1890, and the Seminar Building was built during the Civil War. These were the only old buildings on Main Street to survive "urban renewal" in the 1970s.

THE NASSON COMMUNITY CENTER

THE FOCUS ON CAMPUS now shifted to saving the gym.

In 2001, the Sanford-Springvale Community Center Committee (SSCCC) was organized by Fred Boyle, president of the Sanford-Springvale Rotary Club, and John Black, president of the Sanford-Springvale Youth Athletic Association (SSYAA). The committee also included members of the Rotary Club, the NCAA, Sanford Parks and Recreation, the Springvale Library Association, the Sanford School Department, the University of Maine System-Sanford Center," town officials, and private citizens.[298]

The vision of the SSCCC was to "create a multipurpose center, which encourages community involvement through wholesome family and individual activities by obtaining and revitalizing a landmark facility in the heart of the village of Springvale."[299] The idea was for the SSCCC to accept the gym as a gift from the Springvale Library and to fund its restoration. After the property was acquired, SSCCC's plan was to guide the restoration, renovation, and reopening of the facility to make it a community center for the citizens of Sanford and Springvale. The committee argued that the time was right. Everything was coming together, with the Orlo Williams bequest to the library, the acquisition of the property from Mattar, the razing of the dining commons and Allen Hall, the planned construction of a new courthouse, and the gifting of the property by the library. The committee planned to issue a bond to pay for the project, spreading the cost out over ten years, "allowing for future residents of the community to assist in this endeavor."[300]

---

298 Sanford-Springvale Community Center Committee, flyer, 2001.
299 Ibid.
300 Ibid

Less than a month later, the federal government came through, only this time it was not the Department of Education, but rather the Economic Development Administration (EDA).[301] The EDA granted $500,000 to Sanford-Springvale to provide for air-conditioning in the Anderson Learning Center, to create a parking lot in what used to be the Nasson "quad," and to landscape the area.

On May 10, the committee held an open house in the gymnasium and the Little Theatre. Walking tours were available, and a handout card invited guests to ask questions and see for themselves "the beauty and potential that is available to our community." The public feedback was positive. As one reporter put it, "If you stand in the Springvale gym and close your eyes, you can almost hear [Dizzy] Gillespie blowing his trumpet." Visitors recalled seeing the Portland Symphony Orchestra and a lecture by Harvard behaviorist B. F. Skinner. Over the years there had been dance parties and basketball in the gym, and in the basement was a rifle range, a bowling alley, and a weight room. A chapel was still on the main floor, complete with stained-glass windows.

Backers of the plan wanted the town of Sanford to take over the facility and help fund its renovation. They firmly believed that once restored, the gym could be transformed into the Sanford-Springvale Community Center, a magnet for sports, theater, and other cultural events. While the building was said to be "structurally sound," it needed roof repairs, repairs to the gym floor, new wiring, plumbing, heating, and more—at a total estimated cost of $934,000.

In May 2001, the library offered the gym as a gift to the town.[302] Town-meeting members recommended that the deed be conveyed within six months after satisfactory investigation and approval of all terms and conditions by the Board of Selectmen. The board voted to spend $100,000 to repair the roof and make other critical repairs.

But in August, the board refused to include an article for the town-meeting asking the town to accept the building. At the meeting, there was a crowd of about seventy residents who came to speak in favor of the article. No one spoke against the article, except for Selectmen Gordon Paul, Herbert Stone, and Elizabeth Dupre. Of course, they were three of the five who could actually vote. The dissenters said that questions about the condition of the gym, how it would be used, funding, and other issues had not been answered satisfactorily. The board of selectmen was denounced for not following a mandate from the town-meeting. Critics said the board was

---

301 The EDA is an agency within the US Department of Commerce.
302 "CCC Opts Out of Nasson Gym effort ... For Now," *Sanford News*, January 31, 2002.

charged by the town-meeting to formally accept the building and iron out renovations and financing details. There were procedural arguments—an "emergency article" meant something that developed suddenly, which, some felt, the situation with the gym was not. At a meeting, when one speaker spoke in favor of the gym, he was stopped on a point of order, but as Chairman William Roberts observed, "When I have 150 people applauding for one speaker, I think he's earned the right."

Editorials supported the gym or at least the process that would decide it. Referring to the selectmen's vote against the proposal, an editorial opined that the vote was insulting to supporters of the community center project, whose request it described as "modest." Specifically, the residents were not asking for money or even a commitment, only for permission to have the 147 members of the representative town-meeting clarify a vote they'd taken back in May. Moreover, the vote was insulting to the town's recreation programs, which needed better space. Finally, the editorial speculated that some in town would feel that "the folks who run things at Town Hall would not recognize a good opportunity if it bit them on the nose." In any event, because only issues listed on the warrant are on the official agenda, the SSCCC could not discuss the gym at the town-meeting. The deal was dead.

Consequently, the library voted to put the property up for sale. According to Robert Riding, vice chairman of the library's board of trustees, the library had offered it to the town twice, and it was turned down both times. As a result, SSCCC abandoned its efforts to convince the town to accept the former Nasson gym. Alex MacPhail, a SSCCC member, said the major hurdle was always the overwhelming cost of the project. Still, he said, there were residents who would keep on fighting for it.[303]

MacPhail was right. Shortly after the final town-meeting rejected ownership of the gym, a couple of Nasson alumni began exchanging e-mails, and asked each other, "Why don't we buy it?"

Howard Phillips "Pete" Smith, '72; Rick Schneider, '71; Anna Ashley, '60; and Connie Witherby, '73 had all been active participants in alumni activities over the years. Smith had reinstated the radio station online, Schneider had created the website and yearbook, Ashley was instrumental in creating the Heritage Center, and Witherby had provided financial and other support for many alumni activities. In any event, this was not to be an official action of the alumni association but of a stand-alone organization.

A conversation ensued with Library President Eileen Heald, and

---

303 Ibid.

she agreed to do nothing with the gym until she'd heard back from the alumni.[304] The alumni group met with Heald, Riding, and Roberts on February 2 to discuss their plans.

Word spread quickly around town. At the February 2002 selectmen's meeting, the future of the gym was expected to be a hot topic. When some expressed the belief that the gym was now on the market and was thus a dead issue, Smith responded, "A group of us are at the very beginning stages of exploring ways to save the Nasson Gym. The group is spearheaded by a few Nasson College alumni and others who support fixing up the building. The Springvale Library Board has told us they are willing to consider any plan we might come up with. But they have told us it's important that it happen quickly."[305]

The alumni's plan was to organize a not-for-profit corporation to purchase the facility. The group would ask the library to grant them an option to buy or to lease with an option to buy while the four alumni launched a fund-raising campaign to rehabilitate the facility. The library supported the goal and indicated a willingness to sell it to the group for a dollar—if the group could present the library board with a credible proposal by March 21, 2002.[306]

The story of the alumni's plans broke in the press on February 15, 2002. But also mentioned was another new idea just getting a foothold in town. Town Selectman Herbert Stone suggested the town explore use of another building for a community center, the former Spinelli Cinema located behind Ballenger Auto in Sanford. The cinema property was two and a half acres, including an 11,500-square foot building.

The alumni group's formal proposal was sent to the library on February 23, 2002. Key elements of the plan were as follows:

> Individual alumni of the former Nasson College, along with others, are creating a new not-for-profit corporation, which will apply for status as a charitable organization under Section 501(c)(3) under the Internal Revenue Code ("Buyer"), whereby donations to the organization are tax deductible for the donor.
>
> The Buyer would like to obtain a lease from the Springvale Public Library ("Library") for a period up to one year, at a total cost to the Buyer of one dollar ($1.00). This should be

304 Anna Ashley, e-mail to Richard Schneider, January 21, 2002.
305 Pete Smith, e-mail to Richard Schneider, February 5, 2002.
306 Pete Smith, e-mail to Bjorn Lindgren, February 5, 2002.

a net lease, whereby the Buyer will assume responsibility for insurance (the Library will be named as an additional insured) and maintenance of the property. [The seller] represent[s] that the liability insurance costs approximately $800 per year, that the property is not on the real estate tax rolls, and that there are no outstanding liens or other claims against the property. The Library will provide to Buyer a copy of a survey showing the actual boundary lines of the real property. During the lease period, the Buyer will not sublet the property.

At any time during the lease period, but not later than the end of the one-year lease, Buyer will purchase from the Library, and the Library will sell to the Buyer, at an additional cost of one dollar ($1.00), the fee-simple title to the real property and all the improvements and easements thereon, including the contents of the buildings.[307]

Heald generally approved the proposal, seeking only minor changes. For example, she wanted to make sure that the condition of the property was accepted "as is," noting the possible presence of hazardous materials in the building, such as asbestos, lead paint, and the like.[308] She also wanted to make sure the library was covered by insurance and reserved the right to enter the property at any time during the lease period.

By then, the group had secured more than $30,000 in pledges for the project.[309]

At the same time, the other idea for a community center gym, the former Spinelli movie theater, was still in play. It had its supporters. Elizabeth Dupre noted that the movie theater was off the road and had plenty of parking. She thought it would offer the town something to look forward to and "give the town a lift." In response, Pete Smith, who represented what was now known as Nasson Center Redevelopment Inc.,[310] said that the Spinelli concept had no impact on his group's plans.

Others in town were also unsure that redeveloping the gym was a

---

307 Richard Schneider, letter to Eileen Heald, February 23, 2002 (internal footnotes omitted).

308 Ibid.

309 Connie Witherby, e-mail to Richard Schneider, February 23, 2002.

310 Nasson Center Redevelopment Inc. filed its incorporation papers with the state of Maine on February 15, 2002. The organizational meeting was held on February 28, 2002, at which time Ashley, Smith, Schneider, and Witherby were elected as the initial directors of the corporation. NCR received its initial determination letter

good idea, or even feasible. After a presentation to Nasson alumni on May 5, 2002, Jean Paul, a local resident and an alumna of the college, wrote to Schneider suggesting he and his committee obtain a copy of the comprehensive report that had been presented to the Sanford Board of Selectmen by Mike Ralston, acting town planner.[311] She charged that Schneider had neglected to inform the alumni that the most urgent needs in the building included installation of a complete new water and sewer system, removal of large amounts of lead in the old rifle range in the basement, and replacement of the roof at a cost of $100,000. She thought that the citizens would not support an effort that resembled pouring money down a hole. She agreed with the idea that a community center should be at the center of the community, in other words, in Sanford, which the Nasson gym was not. Most significantly, she noted that Ralston's report recommended that the buildings be demolished and replaced by a park.[312]

Paul's concerns were certainly legitimate, but none of them was seen as insurmountable by the alumni. Negotiations between the library and NCR had their contentious moments. Each side raised concerns about this proposed legal clause or that proposed procedure, and while it took a little longer than expected, success was never in doubt.

Plans were announced to alumni via the website on April 2, 2002, and discussed in detail at Alumni Day on May 6. Schneider simply stated the focus of the concept for the alumni, writing, "This will be the first time since the college closed that alumni will be in control of the future of any part of the old campus. All those years that you and I sat by watching other people make decisions for us were too sad and frustrating. But at last, this project will be wholly owned and controlled by Nasson alumni.[313]

And by the way, added Smith, since we owned the building, there could be various naming rights options for significant donations.

The lease was signed on July 2, 2002. The total rent for one year was one dollar. That was the easy part. The lease required the group to pay for all the utilities and to carry $500,000 in liability insurance. The critical part was "Section 17: Option to Purchase Real Estate." The purchase price would also be only one dollar. But the provision that really mattered was the following:

---

from the Internal Revenue Service approving its 501(c)(3) status on October 11, 2002.

311 Jean Paul, e-mail to Schneider, March 22, 2002.

312 Ibid.

313 Pete Smith, letter to alumni, May 11, 2002.

This conveyance is made expressly conditional upon the Buyer repairing the roofs on the Gym and Chapel wings in a manner to make the same weathertight on or before the expiration of twelve (12) months from the date of this deed and upon further condition that the Buyer obtain a Certificate of Occupancy from the Town of Sanford and/or other controlling governmental authority for any part of the premises on or before the expiration of thirty-six (36) months from the date of this deed. At such time as both of the conditions have been met, Seller shall immediately sign and record in the Registry of Deeds a statement that Buyer has met all of the above conditions and this Reversionary Clause is null and void.

When the deed was issued to NCR on November 1, 2002, the town valued the property, land, and building at only $40,000.

Once the deal was made, the "key to the front door" was handed over to the new owners of the building in a big public ceremony on July 22, 2002. An estimated one hundred people turned out for the formal passing of the keys. US Senator Susan Collins and US Representative Tom Allen also spoke at the event and pledged to help the alumni group search for funding to rehabilitate the building. Organizers handed out T-shirts to kids and bottles of water to adults. The SSYAA would be one of the first tenants of the building, including about 650 kids in its programs. And of great emotional importance, the old proposed name of Sanford-Springvale Community Center was now history. The facility would henceforth be known as the Nasson Community Center

The corporation grew quickly. Peter Faulkner was named general counsel, and the board was expanded. The building committee was chaired by Carl Beal, the fund-raising committee was chaired by Laura Nickerson, and the operations and budget committee was headed by Kevin Langlais.[314]

Work soon got under way. The leaky old roof was removed, and a new *rubber* roof was installed. By that time NCR had raised over $160,000 to renovate the building. An architect drew up plans for a new entranceway and provisions for an elevator to the lower level of the facility.

The first official event of the Nasson Community Center took place on May 3, 2003, not at the gym itself, which was still under renovation, but at Sanford's Goodall Park. This was a benefit concert and barbeque.

---

314 NCR fund-raising brochure, undated.

Four musical groups, including the Pine Hill Ramblers bluegrass band, the Sanford High School Chamber Singers, the Sanford High School Jazz Band, and the Curtis Lake Christian Church Choir performed.

THE DAY SO BIG IT TOOK TWO NIGHTS![315]

For homecoming October 2002, the partying began on Friday night, with a dinner and sock hop at Kevin Shirley's Doo Wop Diner in Springvale, and it went strong until midnight. The Saturday homecoming parade kicked off with the usual high energy, even if the street audience was reduced due to light rain that morning. But just as the parade marchers were beginning to line up for the march around the block, the sun came out, and it turned into a beautiful day.[316]

Back on campus, the dedication of the Nasson Memorial Bench and Walkway at the new Nasson Flag Plaza was held. Speakers included William Hoag, '56; the Reverend Robert Mylod, '60; Robert Stone, '72; Dr. Edward Durnall (former dean of Nasson College); and Alumni Association President Richard Ford, '65. The event concluded with a presentation of an Alumnus Award and a benediction by the Reverend Halsey Stevens, '62.[317]

At the alumni annual meeting, scholarships were awarded to Katherine Plocharczyk and Kristi Cochin. Alumni of the Year recognition went to Dr. Gordon "Bud" Johnston (faculty); June Peterson Gillis, '54; and George Gillis, '55. Marion Smith Sugden, class of 1932, was recognized as the senior alumna in attendance. The yearbook went on sale again, dedicated to former English and drama professor Leonard Whittier.

In the evening, the dinner dance was held off campus at the Sanford American Legion Hall on Main Street between Springvale and Sanford, with entertainment by the Beatles' tribute band, All Together Now.

During the year, the NCAA Recorded History Project interviewed Lisa Cashen, '86, and former Director of Admissions James Coleville. Lisa's interview was especially poignant because she had entered as a freshman in the fall of 1982, right before the school declared bankruptcy. Lisa said that, although she had to finish her schooling at another college, she always regarded Nasson as *her* school.

The Concert Lecture Series, always a popular event back in the days of the college, was restored to activity that year, under the leadership of

---

315 *Nugget*, 2002–2003.
316 Ibid.
317 Program for the event.

George Gillis, '55. Programs included the lecture "Understanding China" by Mathew P. Ward. That was followed by a popular model train display in October and then a concert by "The Music Makers." The winter program was "Lumbering in 19th Century New Hampshire" featuring many tools used in the woods more than one hundred years ago. In April, H. Draper Hunt III presented a lecture called "Rendezvous with Destiny: Eleanor and Franklin Roosevelt, 1887–1921." In May, Breda White spoke on "Al-Andalus: Treasures of Islamic Spain."

The homecoming 2003 weekend kicked off once again at the Doo Wop Diner in Springvale. This time, the rain did not go away for the parade, but that did not stop hardy Nasson alumni from making their march. Adele McCraty Clark, Nasson Institute, class of 1929, was recognized as the senior alumna in attendance. That year's dinner and dance was held at the Potting Shed in Acton.

THE COMMUNITY CENTER OPENS

You're Invited to the

Gala Grand Opening of

the

Nasson Community Center

Saturday, May 1, 2004

7 p.m. to 11 p.m.

It was a long time coming, but on May 1, 2004, the long-neglected, long-debated, and long-desired Nasson Community Center opened for business. The Grand Opening Ceremony commenced at 8:00 p.m. with Alex MacPhail as master of ceremonies, followed by a welcome from H. Pete Smith, president of Nasson Center Redevelopment Inc., who gave a retrospective about making the dream a reality. Letters from various dignitaries were read, including a letter from Congressman Tom Allen and another from Gordon Paul, chairman of the Sanford Town Council. Construction project manager Alan Walsh presented flowers to Anna Ashley, and Allen Mapes gave a history of the gym. Hundreds of people, many dressed to the nines for an occasion the likes of which had not been seen in town in ages, attended. The band played until midnight, an hour past their scheduled time. While there were many people from the area, it was Nasson alumni who partied hardy and closed the place down at about 1:00 a.m.

During the year, the NCAA Living History Project continued, with interviews of Leonard Whittier and Bill Hoag. Rick Schneider stepped down as editor of the *Nugget* after five years, and the job was taken over by Brad French, '74, and Dick Curtis, '61.[318]

New in 2005 was the creation of the Nasson Hall of Fame. At the suggestion of Norm Pulaski, '62, the alumni association established a hall of fame to honor members of the Nasson College family who had distinguished themselves. The three charter honorees were Richard Ford, '65; Anna Ashley, '60; and George McEvoy, '61.

On October 7, 2006, Nasson won a homecoming basketball game for the first time in, well, decades. The final score was 20 to 16, reflecting the special rules used for this basketball game in the Nasson gym (half-court only and shorter game time, to keep the paramedics away). The victory was inevitable, to be sure, as only Nasson alumni were on the two teams. Alumni from even-numbered years competed against a team of alumni from odd-numbered years. Early on, the game was close, but by halftime the odds began to pull ahead and held on to the finish.

On September 16, 2006, alumni of the New Division of Nasson College held a reunion, forty years after the date on which they'd first gathered. About forty-seven members of the group attended, plus lots of significant others. Dinner on Friday was in Kennebunkport, and on Saturday, the group visited the former New Division Campus, now owned by John Barth. While the lower campus was, by then, being rehabilitated and put to new uses, it seemed that any new use of the New Division buildings was still off in the future. Many pictures were taken, with the favorite location being the amphitheater in the back of the original New Division building. That evening included an official "town-meeting," the official form of government of the New Division. All alumni present that weekend were awarded honorary doctorate degrees.

THE LITTLE THEATRE AT NASSON

After the gym was open and running, attention turned to the Little Theatre. The theater did not just need mere renovation but a full reconstruction. The roof was okay, and the building had remained dry all this time. But the

318 The last year of the new *Nugget* was 2006.

building structure had originally been a barn in the mid-1800s. (Really!) Over the decades since—*centuries*, actually—the barn was repeatedly converted to serve one new function after another. It was a livery stable, a blacksmith's shop, and a garage for a local undertaker (he kept his hearse there, one of the first automobiles in southern Maine). In 1937, the building was sold to Nasson, which had grown from institute to college just two years earlier. It was then converted into a recreation hall. It was the school's gymnasium, assembly room, and dance hall.[319] After the Memorial Student Activity Center was built next to it in 1959, it became a lecture hall and part-time theater. After the Science Center opened in 1971, it was converted again, this time into the Little Theatre at Nasson.[320]

Nasson Center Redevelopment decided that the renovation should allow space for nontheater functions, such as receptions, workshops, and small conventions.[321] An advisory committee under the chairmanship of Gary Sullivan was organized in 2004.

There were major hurdles to overcome. Chief among them was the fact that the foundation was still the original rubble rock wall. The floor in the basement was just a dirt floor. Some beams holding up the floor were actually *logs*. Add to that the fact that the building had been basically abandoned for about twenty years. It needed a new electrical system, plumbing, HVAC, and everything else. There was no theater equipment at all, no stage equipment, no lights, and no seats. The projected cost for the theater renovations was expected to be about $200,000.[322]

Groundbreaking was held on July 30, 2007.[323] Community Center President H. Pete Smith said he expected the theater, which he described as the "crown jewel of the Nasson Community Center," would become a center for the performing arts in the Sanford-Springvale area. Alan Walsh, NCC director, said the theater would be "an important anchor in helping to continue economic growth, as well as bringing culture and entertainment to the community." Gary Sullivan, chairman of the Little Theatre renovation committee, envisioned a venue suitable not only for films, lectures, and staged musical and theater performances but also for community events like public speakers, meetings, baby showers, or wedding receptions.[324]

---

319 Based on original research by Albert Prosser.
320 "Will You Be My Angel?" fund-raising brochure.
321 Playbill "Celebration," September 17, 2009.
322 *Nasson News*, Winter 2005.
323 *See* Andrea Rose, "Big Plans, Little Theater," *Weekly Observer*, July 25, 2007.
324 Ibid.

The total estimated cost had by then risen to $360,000, according to Smith.[325]

Michael Ralston became project manager. He and architect David Joy redesigned the structure by adding two rooms on either side. The building was jacked up; the basement was dug out and made deeper. New cement foundation walls were created, with steel columns replacing the old wooden posts, and a finished cement floor was laid. In the auditorium, newly purchased folding theater seats were placed on retractable risers. This way, the seats could be fully extended for theatrical performances or closed up and pushed back, leaving most of the room's flat floor open for table seating for banquets and the like. Construction proceeded expeditiously.

Meanwhile, each spring, a classic educational scene returns to the campus. Seacoast Career Schools, a local school that trains individuals for allied health career opportunities, holds its graduation ceremonies inside the gym. Students attend in caps and gowns, proud parents watch from the audience, a podium is on the stage, and diplomas are handed out.[326]

So near and yet so far.

THE FALL OF EDWARD MATTAR

Whatever became of Nasson's old nemesis Edward P. Mattar III? It seems his dealings in Maine were nothing compared to what he did in Denver.

In 1989, Mattar bought BestBank as a fiftieth birthday present for himself. He became chairman of the board of directors, and in 1995, BestBank was named one of the best-performing small banks in the country by *American Banker*, a national trade publication. In 1997, BestBank reported assets of more than $30 million.[327] By 1998, bank assets grew to $314 million.[328]

Once again, it was all an illusion. In 1998, the bank failed. Mattar and four others were charged with fraud, money laundering, and tax evasion, stemming from what federal prosecutors called a scheme in which they caused the bank to become insolvent by inflating its assets and giving themselves multimillion-dollar bonuses based on those assets.[329] The

---

325 Ibid.

326 Seacoast Career Schools is institutionally accredited by the Accrediting Council for Continuing Education and Training, a national accrediting agency listed by the US Secretary of Education.

327 Mark Shanahan, "Nasson's 'Savior' Writes New Chapter," *Maine Sunday Telegram*, December 14, 1997.

328 www.fosters.com (November 8, 2007).

329 *The Daily Times-Call*, February 19, 2004; *United States v. Gallant*, 2006 WL 278554

indictment consisted of ninety-five counts. Mattar was accused of paying himself more than $5 million in bonuses. According to prosecutors, the bank attracted new depositors by offering above-market interest rates on savings accounts and by issuing about five hundred thousand high-risk credit cards, which eventually resulted in $134 million in losses, but the bank only had about $23 million in reserves for bad debts. The bank was closed and sold by federal regulators in 1998 after it was determined that the bank's liabilities outweighed its assets by more than $200 million. The FDIC later paid depositors more than $170 million to reimburse its insured accounts.

The result? Mattar and two other bank executives were convicted of numerous felony counts of bank fraud and conspiracy. His sentence was expected to be similar to that of one of the other defendants—seven and a half years in federal prison and forfeiture of $4.7 million. But the sentence was never handed down.

For Edward P. Mattar III, whose Nasson College exploits were just one of many unseemly activities throughout his life, it all ended quickly. On November 2, 2007, Mattar used a sledge hammer to knock out a window in his twenty-seventh floor apartment, and jumped to his death. [330]

(D. Colo.).

330 "CNEC Official Plummets to Death," *Telegram & Gazette*, November 3, 2007.

10

THE REST OF THE CAMPUS GETS DEVELOPED

On June 25, 2009, Rob Reinken announced that he had come up with a plan to rehabilitate the 40,000-square foot Science Center.[331] Initially, Reinken replaced the porch on the Oak Street side of the building and installed new stairs and wrought iron railings. The building got new windows, new siding, and new paint. He planned to market it as a business center, and he would rebuild the interior to suit the needs of the businesses that moved in. Reinken applied to the town to have the lot designated as a "Pine Tree Zone," which would make state tax benefits available to qualifying businesses that chose to locate in the center. Pine Tree credits were reported to include tax credits, sales tax exemptions, and payroll tax reimbursements for up to ten years. The beautifully restored building received its first tenants in 2011.

Over at the Anderson Learning Center, the University of Maine System moved out of the space that it had occupied for many years. According to Christine LeGore, director of distance education, economic factors were the reason for the move. That is, enrollment in face-to-face courses had declined over the years, while enrollment in interactive TV and web-based courses had increased.[332] Today, one of the ALC's prime tenants is the University of Maine System's distance education organization, University

---

331 *The Lion Speaks* (alumni newsletter, Summer 2009), citing the *Sanford News* for June 25, 2009.

332 John Diamond, representative of the University of Maine System, "University College at Sanford to Relocate Within the Community," press release, May 19, 2008.

College, which offers access to courses and programs from the seven Maine state universities at more than seventy-five locations and online. More than three thousand Maine residents take courses and work toward degrees at University College outreach centers and sites each semester. Students who choose to take classes at University College typically are older than the traditional college population. ALC is also home to the University of Maine Cooperative Extension.

Moving into UM System's space is the Sanford Community Adult Education school (SCAE), which offers "high quality, lifelong learning opportunities that empower the individual and family to enhance their quality of life."[333] SCAE's Employment Skills Certificate Program (ESCP) helps local people develop new skills and find employment. The ESCP includes certified nursing, general career skills, clerical, administrative assistant, accounting clerk, medical secretary, and medical billing and coding certificates. In June 2010, SCAE awarded forty-nine certificates to thirty students at graduation.

Other tenants in the ALC have included the All Friends Learning Center, the Parent Resource Center, the Business Enterprise Center, the Southern Maine Regional Planning office, Coastal Enterprises Inc., the York County Soil & Water Conservation district office, the PRC Family Access Program, the Grahamtastic Connection, and of course, the Nasson Heritage Center.

Marking another milestone, the Little Theatre had its grand-opening celebration on September 17, 2009. The final cost to renovate the building was $567,652 in cash and $261,980 in in-kind contributions, for a grand total cost of $829,632.[334] The program opened with a greeting by Gary Sullivan and Fred Boyle, remarks by the NCC Board Chairwoman Doreen Warren, and NCC Executive Director Alan Walsh, as well as a thank you from contractor Ron Woodward and other remarks by Little Theatre Committee Chairwoman Lorraine Masure. Lastly, the theater's "christening" was by Sanford Town Council Chairman Joseph Hanslip.

THE 1971 TIME CAPSULE

One surprise popped up. Once again, we go back to the old college. Rick Schneider, who was instrumental in converting the old recreation hall into the Little Theatre at Nasson back in 1971, had been asked to create a time capsule of some sort that would be embedded in a wall in the theater. He

---

333 http://sanford.maineadulted.org. Accessed March 18, 2012.
334 Playbill (September 17, 2009).

did so, putting in it information about the theater, programs of shows, plans for the new design, photographs, and the like. The box was soldered shut and placed in the wall in the theater lobby, behind a plaque that read simply, "1971."

After the school closed, the theater sat vacant. From time to time, rumors circulated that the theater building, among other buildings, was about to be torn down. During one year's homecoming event in the late 1980s or early 1990s, Schneider was able to gain entry into the theater and went after the time capsule. The plaque was screwed to the wall, and Schneider had no tools available. He asked the security person who had let him in if he would wait a few minutes while he ran to the local Rite Aid to buy a screwdriver. When Schneider returned, the building was closed up, and the guard was nowhere to be found. This could be a problem. Before, no one knew there was anything behind that plaque. Now, Schneider had disclosed that there was something of value hidden away. Sure enough, a year or two later, when Schneider was next able to get into the theater, the plaque was gone, and only a hole in the wall where the time capsule had been remained. From time to time, the subject of the box arose among alumni, as people tried to determine who the security guard might have been and what he might have done with it.

Years passed, and never was there any sign or word of what might have happened to the time capsule. So it was quite a surprise when, on the occasion of the reopening of the Little Theatre, Springvale Library trustee Robert Riding presented the old copper box to Peggy Driscoll. How it made its way to the library was never determined. One theory was that Captain Prosser recovered the box when the school closed in 1983, though how it got from him to the library is also a mystery. Another more likely theory is that Dean McLaughlin recovered it around the time the school closed. The box had a note attached to it that said, "Removed from L.T. Cornerstone type box – Contents placed into box on opening of the Little Theatre. Dean Mac." Exactly what McLaughlin did with it all those years is not known. At some point, it seems he gave it to the library.[335] In any event, there it remained until the late 1990s. When the library was undergoing its own rebuilding, the box surfaced. At the time, there was no activity involving the theater, so Riding took the box home and forgot about it until the theater finally reopened.

Homecoming 2009 was a three-day event on October 2 through 4.[336] On Friday evening, there was a group dinner at the Back Street Grill in

---

335 If that's what happened, the box was actually long gone by the time Schneider tried to recover it.

336 *The Lion Speaks* (Summer 2009).

Sanford. On Saturday was morning coffee at the Heritage Center and the annual meeting of the NCAA, but the annual homecoming parade was rained out for the first time. In the evening, there was another grand opening of the theater just for alumni, with an alumni talent show. The weekend wrapped up Sunday morning with bagels and coffee in the Heritage Center.

Homecoming 2010 was another three-day event. The Backstreet Grill had become the gathering place for alumni on Friday night. Saturday included the usual meetings and parade, with an evening concert in the gym. The following year, Homecoming 2011, included all the regular activities, plus a Lion Luau on the quad (or what was left of it).

With plans for Marland Hall to open in the fall of 2012, redevelopment of the original core campus was finally complete, almost thirty years after the school closed.

11

THE MAGIC THAT IS NASSON

WHAT IS IT ABOUT Nasson that keeps this story alive, almost thirty years after the original school went bankrupt and closed its doors? Hundreds of other colleges have closed over the years,[337] and yet it is only *Nasson College* that still draws its alumni and staff back to campus year after year in large numbers.

Indeed, it is not only Nasson graduates who cling to the Nasson memory. Many students who, for one reason or another, never actually graduated from Nasson, still think of Nasson as *their* college and still return for reunions.

The alumni tagline used for many years after the school closed was "The Magic That Is Nasson"—not "The Magic that *Was* Nasson"; for past tense would imply an event that had ended—something over and done with. No, there is still today something magical about the place, and the devotion it inspired in its students.

Some of the explanation for this devotion comes from Richard D'Abate's description of Nassonites in his epilogue in Prosser's book. He wrote, "Many fine students were newly awakened to their abilities while at Nasson; many creative and wonderfully quirky personalities were given room to grow at Nasson; and many affable young people learned how to work hard and take responsibility for themselves at Nasson."[338] Quote this line, and you will see many alumni nod their heads in agreement.

Faculty and staff keep returning too. Many professors and administrators are regular attendees at reunions, not to mention volunteering their time

337 www.closedcolleges.org
338 Prosser and D'Abate, *The Seventy Years*, 182.

and efforts and their abundant knowledge to the affairs of the alumni association and maintenance of the Heritage Center.

And yet, there are reports that some members of the Nasson community, even after all these years, cannot bring themselves to revisit the campus. There are stories of some former staff who actually live within a few miles of Springvale but have never set foot on the campus. Such was the distress caused by the failure and closing of the school decades ago.

Of course, this can't go on forever. The number of alumni shrinks a little more every year. Every announcement of a beloved professor who has passed away leaves their former students in mourning. The loss of classmates reminds everyone of his or her own mortality. The youngest Nasson graduates are now over fifty years old.

In recognition of that inevitable problem, some years back, Alumni President Richard Ford established an alumni endowment fund. The purpose was to ensure that, even after alumni have ceased to remain in sufficient numbers to maintain records and memories of old Nasson College, there would be funds to house and administer the school's legacy.

Let's look at some numbers for perspective—if the school had not closed but maintained a modest student enrollment of, say, 600 students, each year about 150 graduates would join the ranks of alumni. Over the thirty years since the school's closing, that would have meant some *4,500* additional members of the alumni association.

When an alumnus returns to the campus for the first time since graduation, the view is still familiar. The old grassy quad is now a parking lot, and where the dining commons used to be is now a courthouse. Allen Hall is gone too. But the structure of the campus remains. Brown Hall and Alumni Hall are in good shape. The gym, the Science Center, the library, and Marland Hall still frame the main campus. Exteriors are mostly unchanged, and interiors are also pretty much unchanged, just renovated. A couple of million dollars in capital improvements will do wonders. It's not just alumni who valued the campus. It was, after all, mostly townspeople who saved the buildings. Happily, with a nod to tradition, Rob Reinken has retained the names of many of the old Nasson buildings.

The story of the school and the campus since 1983 is a little like *The Perils of Pauline*, the old silent film series about the beautiful girl who is tied to the railroad tracks by the evil villain (always dressed in black), but who is rescued by her love, the hero (always dressed in white) just before the train comes 'round the bend. The college was never rescued, but the campus eventually was, after all the *sturm and drang*. Thus, this story continues with optimism, more than many people expected.

In 2012, the Nasson College family celebrates one hundred years since the founding of the school. It is hard to imagine that even George Nasson himself could have foreseen what his great vision created. And we will be eternally in his debt.

Appendix A:
Sources and Acknowledgments

The foundation for much of the early years of this story came from the court decisions for the numerous lawsuits that involved Nasson College. These are official records, and I generally consider them to be authoritative.

Newspaper articles from the *Portland Press Herald/Maine Sunday Telegram*, the *Sanford News*, the *Journal Tribune*, *The Boston Globe*, and others provided most of the facts of this story. Where available, the specific information of each article is provided.

Additional sources include:

Publications of the Nasson College Alumni Association, official (such as published newsletters) and less official (postcards, letters, and the like)

Publications of (Mattar's) Nasson College, post-1983

Many other pieces of ephemera. These are identified as best as possible. I am especially grateful to Eugene Daly, former professor at Nasson College, for his stewardship of the Nasson College archives in the Heritage Center. The materials there have been a vital resource for this story.

Video histories, created by the NCAA. During the early 2000s, the author, with the assistance of H. Pete Smith, conducted numerous interviews with various people connected with Nasson College, including alumni, faculty, staff, members of the board of trustees, and others.

Interviews with individuals by the author conducted specifically for this publication, and for other assistance. Specifically, I express my appreciation to Anna Ashley, Elaine Bean, John Downing, Jim Elliott, June Gillis, Rosemary Guptil, Meg Hutchins Broderick, Peter Jacobs, David Jagger, Katin Keirstead, Allen Mapes, Steve Morris, Mike Ralston, Robert Reinken, Edgar Schick, Lionel Sevigny, H. Pete Smith, Robert Stone, Connie Witherby, and many others, in less formal discussions.

I thank Ann Carrie Fisher, class of 1983, for her assistance with research for this book. I also thank Robert Stone, class of 1972, who spent countless hours proofreading and suggesting editorial corrections to this manuscript; his expertise was invaluable.

And I thank many other individuals who contributed their time and knowledge to this story.

A word on the citations. As a lawyer, including "citations of authority" comes naturally to me. As a writer of history, including citations made it easier for me to keep track of all the resources that were used in this work. As a side benefit, they provide source material for anyone who might want to read more about something or, perhaps, just check up on me.

With a history such as this, errors of commission and omission are bound to appear. I apologize in advance to anyone affected.

Appendix B:
The Lawsuits and Administrative Decisions

in chronological order

Nasson College v. NEASC, 80 B.R. 600 (1988).

Spring v. Trustees of the Hervey A. Hanscom Trust, Mass. Probate and Family Court, Docket No. 93E-0080 (Mar. 18, 1994).

Key Trust Co. of Maine v. Nasson College, 697 A.2d 408 (1997).

U.S. Dept. of Education, Report of the Inspector General (May 7, 1998).

In the Matter of Nasson Institute, Docket No. 98-69-ST (Dept. of Education Sept. 23, 1998).

United States v. Mattar, 2007 WL 485349 (D. Colo. 2007)

Appendix C:
The Accreditations and Recognitions of Nasson College

From the Nasson College Catalog, 1982:

Nasson College is accredited by the New England Association of Schools and Colleges.

Nasson is a member of the American Council of Education, the American Library Association, the Association of Governing Boards of Colleges and Universities, the College Entrance Examination Board, the Council for Advancement and Support of Education, the Maine Independent Colleges Association, the Higher Education Council for the State of Maine, the Maine Association of Physical Education and Intercollegiate Athletics for Women, the National Association of Intercollegiate Athletics, the National Collegiate Athletic Association, and the New England Association of Schools and Colleges.

Nasson College is a member of the National Association of College Admissions Counselors and subscribes to its Statement of Principles of Good Practice.

The college is also a charter member of the Research Institute of the Gulf of Maine [TRIGOM], a nonprofit corporation established to conduct research and educational projects related to oceanography.

Appendix D:
The Accreditations and Recognitions of (New) Nasson College and/ or Nasson Institute

c. 1990

The Accrediting Council for Continuing
Education and Training (ACCET).

Appendix E:
Presidents of the Nasson College Alumni Association since the Closing of the School

Robert Stone, '72, 1983–1989

Elaine Coughlin Bean, '74: 1989–1999

Richard Ford, '65: 1999–2005

June Peterson Gillis, '54: 2005–2008

Lorraine Dutile Masure, '70: 2008–2010

Constance Witherby, '73: 2010–

INDEX

A

Accrediting Council for Continuing
    Education & Training 34, 40
Air-Tech Inc. 45, 53
Allen, Jack 6
Allen, Tom 87, 115, 117
Ashley, Anna 51, 61, 81, 94, 96, 98,
    104, 111, 112, 117, 118, 132
Association of Independent Colleges
    and Schools 34
Ayer, Gordon 22

B

Bailey, May 106
Baldwin, Sherman 99
Ballenger Auto 112
Barth, John 45, 47, 99, 118
Bartucca, Joe 104, 107
Beal, Carl 115
Bean, Elaine 37, 59, 60, 61, 62, 81, 94,
    98, 132, 136
Beaton, Mary Elizabeth 103
Becker Junior College 10, 16
Bell, Steve 104
Black, John 109
Borgeault, Robert 6, 15
Boyle, Fred 109, 124
Bray, Mike 61, 94
Brennan, Joseph 5, 30
Business Enterprise Center 100

C

Carpenter, Hazen 98, 101
Cashen, Lisa 116
Central New England College 17,
    18, 22
Clark, Adele 117
Cochin, Kristi 116
Cohen, William 55
Coleville, James 116
Collins, Susan 90, 91, 94, 115
Columbia College 16
Corning Community College 24
Curtis, Dick 118
Curtis Lake Christian Church Choir
    116

D

D'Abate, Richard 127
Dale, William 56
D'Allesandro, Lou 35
Daly, Eugene 98, 131
Dictar Associates 19, 99
Doiron, Matt 106
Doo Wop Diner 116, 117
Dostie, Helen King 105
Douglas, Fred 41
Downing, John 59, 60, 61, 62, 132
Down Maine House 37, 105
Driscoll, Peggy 125
Dupre, Elizabeth 110, 113

Durmont, Charlene Romanko 105
Durnall, Edward 107, 116

E

Eastman, Harland 61
Effective Management Systems Inc.
    85, 86
Elliott, Jim 35, 132

F

Faulkner, Peter 115
Ferguson, Bob 96
Finance Authority of Maine 42, 88
Fisher Ann 94, 132
Ford, Richard 95, 96, 98, 105, 106,
    116, 118, 128, 136
Fortin, Dennis 101
French, Brad 118

G

Garner, Richard 105
Gay, Roger 31
Gillis, George 103, 105, 107, 116, 117
Gillis, June 105, 107, 116, 132, 136
Gold, Morton 107
Gorham Normal School 44
Grace, Faye Everett 29
Guptil, Rosemary 38, 132

H

Haines, Julian 89
Hall, Robert 53
Hanscom, Hervey 34, 44, 45, 133
Hanslip, Joseph 124
Hapenny, Sally 94
Heald, David 97
Heald, Eileen 111
Hildreth, Katherine 17
Hoag, Bill 96, 116, 118
Hoag, Natalie 98, 104
Hoar, C. Scott 97
Holt, Barbara 22, 29, 30, 36

Holtwijk, Theo 57
Howard, Brian 10
Husson College 45, 46
Hutchins, Meg 59, 62, 94, 107, 132

J

Jacobs, Peter 132
Jagger, David 132
Job Training Partnership Act 6, 7
Johnson, Frederick 12
Johnston, Bud 107, 116
Joseph Finn Co. Inc. 14

K

Kearns, Mark 38
Keirstead, Katin 132
King, Heather McNivin 106

L

Langlais, Kevin 115
LeGore, Christine 123
Lenox School 45
Lesley College 24
Libby, James 87
Lillie, Mark 104
Lindgren, Bjorn 112
Longanecker, David 91
Longfellow, Janice 104
Longley, Andrew 22
Lovegrove, Bob 34

M

MacKinnon, Bruce 87
MacPhail, Alex 111, 117
Maher, Bernard 12
Maine Stage Company 28
Mallanik, Judy 106
Mapes, Allen 4, 22, 31, 55, 57, 86, 98,
    101, 106, 107, 117, 132
Market Decisions 50
Masure, Lorraine 9, 124, 136

Mattar, Edward 17, 18, 19, 20, 21, 22, 23, 34, 36, 38, 40, 41, 42, 46, 48, 49, 54, 55, 56, 85, 86, 87, 88, 89, 90, 91, 92, 93, 96, 97, 98, 99, 101, 109, 120, 121
Mazzaglia, Frank 24, 29
McEvoy, George 118
McLaughlin 22
McLaughlin, James 14, 22, 29, 31, 43, 125
McLaughlin, Philip v
Miles, Michael 99
Miller, David 9, 12, 23, 30
Moore, Savery 104, 107
Morin, Judith 34
Morris, Steve 3, 8, 17, 21, 22, 107, 132
Mylod, Robert 116

N

Nason, Ernie 94
Nasson Center Redevelopment Inc. 114, 115
Nasson Community Center 119, 124
Nasson, George 17, 61, 95, 129
Nasson Heritage Center ix, 81, 94, 95, 124
Nasson Institute 39, 88, 90, 95, 106
Nasson University 90
New Division 19, 37, 99, 118
New England Association of Schools and Colleges (NEASC) 4, 13, 19, 21, 32, 33, 34, 133
Nickerson, Laura 115
Normans 37, 105
Noyes, Howard 22

O

O'Brian, Alice 10
Olson, Majorie 106

P

Paul, Gordon 110, 117
Penta, Don 105

Perry, John 99
Perry, William 24, 31
Plocharczyk, Dave 59
Plocharczyk, Katherine 116
Poulis, Richard 10
Prosser, Albert 43, 95, 119, 125
Prosser, Marion 94, 103, 106
Pulaski, Norman 105, 118

R

Ralston, Mike 55, 57, 114, 120, 132
Ray, Ken 56, 86
Read, Bruce 85
Reinken, Robert 53, 63, 86, 101, 123, 128, 132
Ricker College 12
Ricker, Frank 106
Riding, Robert 111, 125
Riley, Richard 87
Roberts, William 97, 111
Roker, Al 107
Ross, Amy Stevenson 105
Ross, Wayne 5

S

Sanford High School Chamber Singers 116
Sanford High School Jazz Band 116
Sanford-Springvale Community Center Committee (SSCCC) 109, 111
Sanford-Springvale Development Corporation (SSDC) 57, 60, 61, 94, 97
Sanford-Springvale Mousam Way Land Trust 53
Sanford-Springvale Youth Athletic Association (SSYAA) 109, 115
Schick, Edgar 3, 132
Schneider, Richard 59, 62, 89, 90, 91, 94, 95, 98, 103, 104, 106, 107, 111, 112, 114, 118, 124, 125
Scott, Allen 105

Senning, Calvin 22
Sevigny, Lionel 86, 97, 98, 101, 132
Sevigny, Margaret 22
Shirley, Kevin 116
Simpson, Paula 100
Smith, H. Pete 103, 104, 105, 111,
    112, 113, 117, 119, 131, 132
Snowe, Olympia 87, 91
Southern Maine Regional Planning
    Commission 101
Southern Maine Technical College 45
Spinelli Cinema 112
Springvale College 43, 46
Springvale Library 97, 98, 109, 112,
    125
Springvale Redevelopment
    Corporation (SRC) 101
Springvale School 100
Stahlberg, Lawrence 30
Stephens, Les 5
Stevens, Rev. Halsey 116
Stone, Herbert 110, 112
Stone, Robert 1, 29, 30, 37, 59, 94,
    104, 105, 106, 107, 116, 132,
    136
Sugden, Marion 103, 116
Sullivan, Gary 51, 119, 124
Sweetser Children Services 98

T

TDC 5, 6, 7, 11, 15, 19
Tetro, Charles 7
Thomas College 107
Training and Development
    Corporation 5, 6, 7, 15
Tuft's College 44

U

Unity College 31
University of Maine System 4, 45, 46,
    54, 109
University of New England 45, 46,
    59, 60, 61, 62

University of Southern Maine 3, 44

V

Van Buskirk, Lloyd 11
Vic Remy's 37, 105

W

Walsh, Alan 117, 119, 124
Warren, Doreen 124
Webb, Jack 97
Web-NCY 104
Whittier, Leonard 105, 116, 118
Williams, Orlo 97, 109
Windsor, Michelle 61
Winton Scott 49
Winton Scott Architects 49
Witherby, Connie 62, 104, 111, 132,
    136
WNCY-FM 104
Woodberry, Bob 3
Woodward, Ron 124
Worcester Junior College 18

Other works by the author:

The Theater Management Handbook, Richard E. Schneider
& Mary Jo Ford, Betterway Books, Cincinnati, Ohio, 1999

The Well Run Theatre, Richard E. Schneider & Mary
Jo Ford, Drama Books, New York, NY, 1993